Life is Hard

is

Hard

...here's some help

LIFE IS HARD

...here's some help

Virginia Braden
First edition
Amanda Mary, Designer
Nick Ziedler, Photographer
Design elements created by
Visnezh - Freepik.com

THIS BOOK IS dedicated with love to every soul who has ever feared they are not enough and to every spirit that has become weary of bearing that weight. May you find within these pages the courage to awaken to the memory of who you are, and in that remembrance may your soul find its depth and know it's worth. May you know the sanctuary you seek is bathed fully in the brilliance of who you are...

OUR SOULS CRAVE a love that we have somehow come to believe is only available to the perfect, the beautiful, or the lucky. We hide our true selves hoping we can trick the system and somehow qualify to be loved. In doing so we spend most of our lives chasing something that already belongs to us.

You came into this world knowing you had infinite value and worth, and you knew you were worthy of love. Events since then may have convinced you otherwise, but it has never ceased to be truth. You have lived knowing there was more for you while fearing it was out of reach because of what you have perceived to be defects in you. You've heard the cry of your soul again and again to return to its full brilliance, but have believed you were not worthy to shine. Yet even in the darkest shadows your fears and insecurities have cast, hope has dared to dance, beckoning you to abandon your fear and awaken to the joy of who you are.

When you are ready to remember who you really are, absolutely anything is possible. This book is about finding your way back to who you forgot you were and allowing that knowledge to transform your life, liberate your soul, and unleash your brilliance.

Let the journey begin.

HOW TO USE THIS BOOK

This book contains 365 contemplations which are simply engaging thoughts designed to connect with and stir your authentic self. For each contemplation there are exercises to help you integrate the truths into the reality of your world, empowering and encouraging you in meaningful and significant ways. No matter what your current situation or circumstance, within these pages you will find a source of soul shifting inspiration and deep inner healing to draw upon again and again.

There is no right or wrong way in which to read this book. You can start at the beginning and progress through the book in the order it is laid out, or simply open the book each day and trust you will be led to the contemplation you most need that day. You are free to experience this book in the way that is most meaningful to you. Know with each page you turn, we travel this road together, and you are never alone.

Love and Light and Peace be with you Always,

Virginia

Truly the light is sweet, and a pleasant thing
it is for the eyes to behold the sun.

Ecc 11:7

On the other side of the mountain in your way is a stronger, wiser, more confident you wondering why you ever doubted you could make the climb.

If there were one thing your present self would need to hear from your future self right here, right now, what would that be? Write it in the space below.

Hope is not a quiet timid thing. It screams in the face of loss, rages against forecasts of failure, charges at the oncoming night.

What does your hope scream?

Finding and becoming the person you are meant to be means letting go of the person others think you are meant to be.

In the space below write yourself a permission slip to be the person it is you truly wish to be. Get specific. Go all out. Your voice is the most influential voice in your life so make it crystal clear what it is you are giving yourself permission to do and be.

There is a time for whispered soliloquies and hushed prayers and a time when all of heaven and hell needs to hear your battle cry.

What is your battle cry? What are you fiercely in search of with a desperation and an intensity that wells up from within and refuses to be still? What does your heart long for, your soul ache for? What roars within you? Be specific. Listen to the fire within you and let it shape the words you write below.

Wonder is found by simply awakening to the thousands of tiny miracles that surround us at any given time.

Name some tiny miracles present with you now.

You are enough. Always.

You cannot gauge your worth by the successes and failures of your efforts, but by an awareness that you are inherently valuable with a voice and vision unlike any other. You, my friend, are unrepeatable.

Make a list of three circumstances which are invoking a sense of unworthiness and insecurity. For each of those circumstances write: "Even though _____ is occurring in my life, I trust that I am enough." Today each time any of those situations cause you to doubt yourself, remind yourself to practice seeing those situations through the eyes of someone who is enough. What would someone who is enough do, think, or say? Do that and return here to write about your experiences.

The night is a liar, an illusionist at best, pretending power it cannot possess. It is slave to the dawn, no matter its boast.

When we are in crisis the night can seem endless. How can a faith in the dawn's return impact your thoughts and actions today? Write your thoughts below.

Obstacles do not prevent us from reaching our destination. It is our willingness to surrender our progress to them that stays us.

Draw a picture below of yourself next to an obstacle you are facing at this time. Which is larger? Why?

Eliminate shame from your life like it's a plague. It is.

In what way can you actively deny shame a place in your life today?

The obstacles that scare us most are the very same obstacles which impart a confidence not gained any other way.

They are there not to hinder you, but to promote you.

Any courage that is required from you in the process will be returned to you in confidence when the battle is done.

Any task becomes easier with repetition and exposure. What can seem daunting at first becomes second nature with passing time and experience. The new task soon becomes part of our repertoire of things we have mastered.

Think back to a time you had to learn something new and difficult. Remember how awkward it felt? As time passed and you became more familiar with the process, how did your perception of that task as difficult begin change? As you take on current difficulties in your life, be mindful of this principle. In the space provided, list some qualities about you that have enabled you to succeed in the past. How might some of those serve you now with current difficulties?

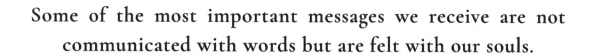

Some of the most important messages we receive are not communicated with words but are felt with our souls.

When is the last time you took the time to listen to what your soul was saying? Take some time right now. Write down your impressions below.

Says who?

Give yourself permission to doubt the "experts". Write about it below.

You can only do what only you can do. Do that and then do more of that.

List three things that only you can do. Promise your future self you will continue to do those things.

Confidence doesn't come from knowing you will win. It comes from knowing, whatever the outcome, you have given it your all and you will be ok.

Think back to a time when the outcome wasn't what you wanted. Thank your former self for the effort he or she gave in pursuit of that outcome. What does it feel like to be proud of the effort you gave regardless of the outcome? Now list one thing you learned as a result of that experience.

Whether traveling in darkness or in light, your journey is yours.

Treasure it.

Name one treasure found in your current journey.

You are loved. Undeniably, irrefutably, unconditionally loved. Period.

As you go throughout your day, remind yourself you are loved as you are. How does this knowledge empower you? How does it change the way you see others? The way you treat others? Be specific.

With every breath you take, fully live your story. You're the only one who can.

What role do you play in your own story? Artist, Hero, Victim, Second String, Architect, Drama Queen? Write about it below.

Yes, you. Of course you! Who else could achieve this dream except the one it has been given to?

Are you willing to consider that this might be true for you? If it were true, how it would change your thoughts, your perspectives, your attitudes, and your actions today?

Write an example of something you would do differently today if this were, in fact, true for you.

Give your dreams full HD color.

Pick a scene, any scene from any part of a dream that you have for your life. Write about it as though you were describing it to someone who cannot see and who is depending on you to describe every little detail and nuance of the scene from your dream.

Talk, think, and act today the way you would if you had already achieved your dreams.

Select one situation in your life that is causing you discomfort or anxiety. Now act as though you have already achieved your dream and write below about how that person would respond to the situation that is causing you stress.

Each day do at least one thing your future self will thank you for.

What one thing could you do today that your future self would be grateful for? Write about it, then do it.

You will fall, you will fail, you will get it wrong, you will miss the mark. It is inevitable. How you respond to those moments tells the story of who you are and who it is you can become.

Name one person you know personally or just know about who has experienced failure but who persevered and, in the end, experienced great success.

Spend at least 5 minutes a day in quiet reverence of the world and its insistence that you be in it.

Set a timer on your phone or alarm clock for five minutes and, in quiet awareness, contemplate the thought that the world needs you, specifically you, right here, right now.

Inspect your beliefs on a regular basis. Question them. Turn them inside and out. They are the most powerful tool you possess and it matters where they are taking you.

Do your current beliefs support you getting where it is you most want to be? How or how not?

Forgiving yourself does not remove the mistake but it shows you know the difference between who you are and what it is. You are not a mistake, your actions sometimes are. Forgiveness sets the record straight and allows you to move forward into the future with head held high.

If there is a mistake you are still clinging to, decide now to let it go. In the space below, write a letter of forgiveness to yourself. Bury the mistake, keep the lesson, and move on.

We so often spend our present minutes in the futile exercise of hoping for a better past.

Intellectually we know we cannot go back in time and change what has been, but emotionally we can find ourselves consumed by the ghosts of what should have or could have been. These illusions are dangerous because they spin a tale that says we cannot have a good future because we have had a less than perfect past.

In the space below, write a list of some disappointments you have faced which still haunt you. Give yourself permission to accept the situations as they are, as less than perfect and less than what you had hoped for. Next, summon great compassion for yourself, acknowledging how difficult it has been to contend with the finality of those moments. Sit with this feeling of compassion for yourself and thank yourself for the great strength you have shown thus far.

Now picture those moments as huge boulders which have been attached to you with thick ropes, preventing you from moving forward into a beautiful future. Give yourself permission to cut the ropes one by one. Feel the weight get lighter and lighter with each rope you cut. Notice the great relief as the last rope is severed and that final bit of weight lifts from you. Take a deep full breath and push your shoulders back. Raise your head high and exhale slowly. You are free.

People will misunderstand you, underestimate you, reject you.

People will also wholeheartedly love and support you, sacrificially give to you, and be there in your darkest moments to remind you that you are loved. You get to decide who and what behaviors you will give your thought, time, and energy to.

What are some things you can choose to remove your attention from today? What are some things you can choose to give your focus to today?

Seek to add value to the world and success will find you.

Take a minute to appreciate what of value you bring to the world, no matter how small. Below, write about how that makes a difference in the lives of those to whom you choose to give those things.

Nothing is worth surrendering your peace. Nothing. No circumstance, no "what if", nothing that has been, and nothing that will be.

How can you protect your peace today?

You can spend your life afraid of monsters that may or may not appear or you can move forward trusting you will be given what you need regardless.

Look back over your journey. Write about a time you were afraid of a monster that never actually came to be, or one that did, but was not nearly as fierce as you had feared it would be.

Every hero needs a villain. That situation you think came to take you out came to prove you are the hero you've been waiting for.

If this situation came to prove you are the hero in your own story, and able to rescue yourself, what would that look like?

Quit praying to be rescued. Pray instead for the vision to see the resources, strength, creativity, and capabilities you already possess. Then pray for the wisdom and understanding to know how to apply them, and the courage to do just that.

Write your own prayer below. Be specific about your situation.

Keep going. Someone else needs the trail you're blazing, the footprints you're leaving.

Consider for just a few moments, that the struggles you are currently facing are paving the way for someone else to find their way home. What are some tips you could give them?

Lead with courage and follow it with up with persistence. Battles aren't won by being brave, they are won by being brave consistently.

What small but courageous action can you take every single day for the next 30 days?

Limitations do not appear to confine us but to point us to the areas where we are most meant to experience growth. Our greatest fears point the way to the places we are meant to experience our greatest victories.

What areas of future victory are your fears pointing to? List them below.

There comes a point in every battle where one can no longer afford the luxury of looking to what was but must focus fully on what lies ahead.

Today, commit to one thing you will do to demonstrate you are removing your focus from what was and placing it on building what is to come. Name that one thing below.

To bear the darkness in the absence of light is courage. To believe light will again return is faith. To have someone wait with you is love.

Name someone who has waited with you in the darkness. Write a letter, an email, send a text, or make a call to them today to let them know how much that meant.

The lie you believe becomes your truth. The walls you build to guard it, your prison.

If there is an area of your life where you feel you are imprisoned, what lie masquerading as truth has put you there?

Pursue your dreams with everything in you. They are meant for you and you for them.

You are the keeper of your dream. It depends on you for life and breath. What energy are you directing to it today? Be specific. Write your thoughts in the space below.

Freedom is defined in what I will no longer allow to define me.

List some labels today that you have worn that you are no longer willing to wear.

Most who have changed the world simply decided it was far less difficult to believe change could occur than to accept it could not.

What condition in your life, in your relationships, in your world are you no longer willing to accept? What are you willing to do today to begin the transformation?

What excuse would you have to give up today to be the person you say you want to be?

Write about how you will act differently today after having given up that excuse.

I cannot blame those things which rob me of my peace for its departure but only myself for my willingness to allow it to go.

What circumstances are you allowing to take your peace? Are they worth it?

Compassion towards yourself will change more than all the "shoulding" and shaming in the world ever could.

Each time and every time you find your inner judge piping up today, answer back with your inner encourager. Let him or her speak loudly and with great compassion. Let him or her acknowledge firmly your imperfections are not fatal, and your flaws are not in the way of your destiny. Let him or her remind you that you, and all your imperfections and flaws, are deeply and thoroughly loved.

Write below: "I will never be perfect AND I will always be of great value and worth. I will never be perfect AND I will always be loved. I will never be perfect AND I will always be enough. "

We often spend so much time avoiding the pain and discomfort of our mistakes that we miss the lesson in them.

Search the painful parts of your journey. Suspend any feelings of guilt or blame and deny shame a place. With full understanding that you are unconditionally loved, ask yourself what gift might there be for you in those painful experiences?

It's not a mistake if you learned from it. It's an education that leaves you in a better place than where you started.

List ten ways your life would be different today if Thomas Edison had allowed his thousands of failures in creating a working light bulb to be the end of the story.

Your life is reconfigurable, built for re-adjustments and recalculations. Translation: you are free at any time to change your mind.

Is there a decision you have made at some point in time that no longer serves you? What decision are you now ready to make? What one step could you take today towards that?

You're stronger, more capable, and braver than you think.

We are often put in touch with our true strength when faced with a situation that forces us to employ new ways of thinking and being. Think back to a time when a circumstance catapulted you out of your comfort zone. What did you learn about yourself in that process? How can you build on the things you learned to help you with today's challenges? Write your thoughts below.

Others can offer counsel and encouragement but there comes a time when we each must find within ourselves the courage to believe and the strength to move.

What thing can you do that only you can do today to step towards your dream?

Those willing to believe in solutions in the face of evidence to the contrary, and with the courage to act on that belief, usually find them.

What action can you take today to stretch towards a solution? Write that down. Now imagine you've reached a solution. How does that make you feel? Write about how it feels to finally have arrived at a solution. Who will benefit from this situation being resolved successfully? What lessons can you take from the journey to help the next time around?

Once you've decided you're not the kind of person who stays down, getting back up simply becomes part of who you are.

Name three times you got back up after falling down. What did you learn about yourself? About life? About others? How does this information help you now?

We move to protect what we value. If you value your status as a victim, you will move to protect it. If you value your status as a champion, you will move heaven and earth to protect it. Each day ask the question: "What version of myself am I protecting?"

What version of yourself are you protecting? Is that version of you one that serves you well?

There is far too much judgment and not nearly enough grace in a world where no one is exempt from falling down. Be about the healing.

To whom can you intentionally show grace and compassion to today?

Circumstances can't define you. Your past has no power in the present. You are who you choose to believe you are. Choose well.

Find a space where it is quiet and ask yourself who you most need to believe you are to reach your destiny. Write down the top qualities of that version of you. Let those qualities guide your decisions and shape your behaviors and responses today and moving forward into the days to come.

Toxic is toxic no matter how well it is dressed or how brightly it smiles.

Where is toxicity hiding out in your life? Decide to get rid of it today.

You cannot make time. We all have just 24 hours in each day. You can, however, take the time to make certain things a priority within those 24 beautiful spaces for opportunities we call a day.

Where do you most need to direct your time, thoughts, energies, and love today?

Your life is making and remaking itself as you read this in a constant ongoing process that is never-ending. It is comprised of what you believe, what you are thinking, and where and with whom you are investing your time, love, and energy.

Take comfort in the beauty of life's seasons and be intentional about surrounding yourself with positive people and healthy environments. Take a minute now to appreciate some of the beautiful things present in your current season. Write your thoughts in the space below.

The courage to openly live our imperfect story is a rare thing. It means being vulnerable. It means opening yourself up to being hurt, misunderstood, and judged. It is also the only way to know true love. Life altering, soul charging, world-changing love.

Have the courage to live YOUR story.

Resist the temptation today to live for the approval of others. Remind yourself how thankful you are for the things that make you who you are. Write down some of those qualities below.

Perfectionism is a bully. It demands everything and gives nothing in return.

In what areas of your life are you being bullied by perfectionism? Name one way you can show yourself love with imperfection in full and plain view?

You create your reality with every breath you take, thought you think, and word you speak. And you are free at any given time to create something different or expand on something you really love.

As the artist of who you are, you not only have the power to, but you have the right to, shape and mold your character, your responses, your perspectives. Write down one specific way this understanding can be of help to you today.

True acceptance is not the absence of accountability but the grace to embrace it.

Make sure there is at least one person in your life who can offer you a safe place to process your anger, fears, doubts, and missteps. Someone who will listen to you at your worst while never losing sight of who you are at your best and who has no problem reminding you of who that best self is.

If you have someone like that, reach out today and let them know how much you appreciate them. If you don't have someone like that in your life today, make it a top priority to cultivate that kind of relationship and don't stop until you have it. In the space below write down some qualities you are looking for in a safe person to process life's ups and downs with.

The darkest parts of our journey are where we become most acquainted with the light inside of us.

Whatever dark places you are facing, know they come to introduce you to the light inside of you. Take a few moments and reflect on how you can bring your light to the dark places you encounter. Write them down and refer back to them often. Know you were created with everything it takes to succeed.

Joy is a choice. Love is a choice. Persistence is a choice. Forgiveness is a choice. Whatever else you don't have, you always have a choice.

Even when we are powerless to change circumstances, we still have the power to choose our responses and how we will treat those around us. Make the conscious decision today to show kindness to another person. Whether a stranger or old friend, choose to give the gift of a kind word, a smile, a simple but sincere gesture, with the expectation of nothing in return. Exercise your power to choose. Write down some qualities you are looking for in a safe person to process life's ups and downs with. Return to this space to record your experience.

When you give your dreams the gift of your fullest and fiercest imagination, a better future is not only possible, it is unavoidable.

Find a quiet place and set a timer for five minutes. Choose a circumstance in your life that you authentically desire to improve. Imagine the very best possible outcome and give it full color and detail. Imagine what it will feel like to have that situation transformed. What will you do differently? How will you feel? How will you celebrate? What will you do with this new reality?

Life comes packaged in possibilities and wrapped in opportunities that rarely resemble what we think they should. Don't let your expectations of what the opportunity should look like keep you from walking through the open door.

Ask yourself honestly, are there opportunities you are overlooking because they don't look like what you thought they would? Write about this below.

It is common to feel fear, to feel inadequate, to feel unworthy. What is uncommon is to choose to wholeheartedly pursue the longing of your soul anyway.

What does your soul long for? How can you pursue that today?

Get rid of "should".

"Should" is an expectation that often locks us into rigid immobility. We often spend so much time fighting for the way something "should" be that we are blind to our power to choose another way. Set aside your shoulds today and look for alternate options. Choose the ones that most resonate with you and which move you forward. Return to this space to record your experience.

Hope shouldn't be the last thing you hold onto, it should be the first.

What are some things you are hoping for today? Why do those things matter to you? Can you allow your hope for those circumstances to empower positive choices today? Write your thoughts below.

Never allow your current circumstances to dictate your destination.

What present circumstances are you allowing to limit your future?
Write them down below.

Commit to a new understanding of those circumstances as necessary parts of your journey which ultimately will help you reach your destination rather than prevent you from reaching your destination. Give thanks for their presence and look forward to their transformation.

Our scars bear witness to more than the wars we've known. They speak of our willingness to be vulnerable in the pursuit of something greater.

Today speak kindly to yourself. All throughout the day remind yourself of good choices you've made. Of your willingness to pursue the dreams written on your heart. Thank yourself for making these choices and for being willing to fall down in order to learn how to get back up.

Burdens don't appear so we can learn to carry them but so we can learn to let them go. Not to weigh us down but to teach us how to be free.

The act of letting go and trusting is one of the most difficult things to do. It means relinquishing control to a power greater than ourselves and trusting we will be cared for. What burdens do you need to let go of today?

Through loss more so than through gain, through heartache even more than through joy, we have learned who we are & to trust in unfailing love.

Whatever season you find yourself in, today make the conscious choice to trust that you are loved with an unfailing love. Let this love guide your thoughts and inform your choices. Let it flow out of you to those around you. How can you express this love to yourself today? How can you express this love to others today? Write your thoughts below.

Let every doubt give way to peace and every question dissolve into hope. You're in this battle to know victory, let no one tell you otherwise.

It is possible to feel stressed and worried and still choose to be hopeful about the future. We may not be able to eliminate fear, but we can acknowledge we feel other things as well and allow the positive emotions to drive our choices. What one thing can you move forward on in spite of feeling afraid?

Adversity introduces us to the very best of who we can be when we choose to see it as friend rather than foe.

Thinking back over your life can you recall a time when a difficult situation resulted in positive growth in your life? Write about what benefits came from that adversity and how they have served you in different situations.

Significance is not a goal to be achieved but the acceptance of who you already are.

Does your life show you know you are significant, important, necessary as you are or are you waiting until you achieve this goal or that goal to make you feel important? What specific external circumstances are you waiting to achieve before you allow yourself to feel important and necessary?

Fill in the blanks:

When I _____ then I will be significant.

When I _____ then I will be important.

When I _____ then I will be worthwhile.

Ask yourself:" Am I willing to continue to give my worth away to these external measurements?

Life is simpler when you realize we're all after love, acceptance, and belonging. Life is meaningful when you choose to give those things.

As many times today as you can, choose to give love, acceptance, and approval to those you come into contact with. Write about your experiences here.

When thoughts of who you should be give way to thoughts of who you could be, the real adventure is about to begin.

What messages are keeping you small? Where did they originate? Why are you giving your belief to them? What one small step can you take today to remove your faith from those statements and live "BIG"?

The fiercest monsters dwell mostly in our minds. We create them, give them life, believe they are real, and so they are.

Describe some monsters you fear.

What qualities are you giving to them? What power have you assigned them? Can you see how you have given life to them? What stories are attached to these monsters? Now, write a story where you realize the monster was nothing more than a figment of your imagination and the worst case scenario nothing more than a dramatic storyline your fears wrote. Write about how you woke up from fear's dream and realized your own strength and ability to write a different story.

A lot of things in this life can be taken from you. Your ability to choose peace, gratitude, love, and forgiveness are not among them.

Name an area or two where you have no options or have faced a loss of control. Now name five things you can choose to do today in any area of your life at all and give all of your focus and energy to doing those five things.

In the sacred space created by our willingness to believe in what could be, grows the courage to pursue it.

Have a conversation with yourself today about how incredible the version of your future you are dreaming of is going to be. Tell yourself how wonderful it will be when you get there. Let yourself know you are willing to learn whatever you need to learn to create this new future. Lastly, tell yourself you are committed to enjoying the journey there and start by writing down one thing in your life that you are satisfied with today. Give thanks throughout the day for this one thing and fully appreciate its presence in your reality.

Far too often we surrender our energy to reflecting on who we've been instead of investing it in developing who it is we want to become.

Name a few things you don't know how to do that you need to know how to do in order to achieve your dreams. Now brainstorm who you could get in touch with that could connect you to that knowledge. Write down their names and commit to reaching out to them by the end of the next 48 hours.

We can get so caught up in assessing the size of a storm that we forget the only thing of significance is who we choose to be in the storm.

Name three things about you that are truly wonderful and that you personally admire. Write about how those characteristics can guide you through any storms you are currently facing. Remind yourself that you were created to succeed and commit to seeing yourself as capable of success.

We've all got broken places, some are just a little more obvious than others. We need less judging, more grace. Less pointing, more lifting.

Who can you lift up today?

Make friends with those things you fear most. Get comfortable in their presence and you will understand they have no real power to harm you.

Pinpoint one thing you are afraid of. Now think of the ways you could respond even if that one thing were to happen. The resources you could gather, the people you could reach out to, the connections you could count on, the options for navigating that situation.

Complete this thought: "Even if _____ were to happen, I know that I could _____ and _____ and _____ and ultimately I would make it through that event and life would continue on.

To see the possibilities in people and in circumstances you must first lay down your prejudices.

Be mindful today of stereotypes, of boxing people and circumstances into pre-configured limitations. Today, approach one person you would never normally take the time to talk to and get to know a little bit about them. Record your experience below.

In a world that is consumed with perfection, it is the courage to be vulnerable that exposes our capacity for true connection.

Where can you lay down the shield of perfection and allow your true, imperfect, and courageous self to shine today?

Develop a picture of what it would look like to win. No matter how unlikely, review it time and again until it becomes the only possibility.

Create a Polaroid image in your mind of what winning would be like for you. Access that image again and again. Write down any thoughts about that image.

Every step, however small, is progress.

Celebrate the small steps today as though they were big steps. Let your body, mind, and emotions fully absorb the fact that progress was made. Write a note of congratulations to yourself below, making sure to list the actual steps you took and giving yourself credit for having taken action.

Emotions are not facts.

Cross-examine a negative emotion you have about a situation today. Hold it accountable for the story it is telling. Is the story true? If so, is it always true? Is the outcome set in stone? Are there really no other options besides the narrative that emotion is creating? What are the actual facts of the situation? Write your thoughts below.

Honor all parts of who you are but be very careful who it is you let occupy the driver's seat.

Imagine a big round conference table in your mind. Fear is there, Joy is there, Hope is there, your Inner Critic is there, your Inner Encourager is there. Let them all have a voice, let them all have a say. Now decide who you will let guide your actions and choices today.

It is one thing to be humble. It is another thing altogether to devalue who you are. You were created to shine. Own that.

The next time someone gives you a compliment, accept it with a smile and acknowledge how much the words mean to you. Part of learning to shine is learning to gracefully acknowledge when someone is touched by your light.

Everything that lies behind you has prepared you for what lies ahead of you. It all works for your good.

We all carry with us a backpack for the adventure of life. Take a few minutes and take an inventory of what is in your backpack. Consider how these resources, tools, beliefs, and experiences can be of service to you now. Get rid of anything in your backpack that does not serve you well.

The pictures you paint with the words that you speak create moments that arrive as your reality. Speak life. Speak faith. Speak hope. Always.

In the space below write down some words of life, faith, and hope over your future and over your present. Now speak them aloud. If possible, record them on your phone or other device and play them any time you start to feel discouraged.

There is perhaps no more critical a response when facing a challenge than to choose to believe you can be the person it takes to overcome it.

We so often identify with the things and qualities we feel we are lacking. We are able to compose lists of what is wrong with us at a much faster rate than lists of what is right with us. Today, focus on what is right with you. Make a list in the space below of five qualities you possess that you identify as strengths and see as assets. How can those qualities help you with a current challenge you are facing? Write down your answers below.

Be adaptable.

Name one way you can make an adjustment today. Give thanks for your ability to course correct, re-direct, and re-appropriate energy.

Of course you don't fit in. You were created to carve out a space all your own.

It is impossible to reach your full potential while carrying the weight of other's approval and disapproval. Their opinion is just that--their opinion.

What would happen if you quit looking for signs of approval everywhere you went and instead brought your loving and unconditional approval to those situations, people, and places? Write your thoughts below.

Your true point of power is not found in achieving a perfect existence but in leveraging the imperfections.

Don't waste time being insecure. You will fail, you will make mistakes—why waste energy and time worrying about when and where those things will occur? Instead, put the energy and time into implementing the lessons learned from previous missteps. Prove to yourself you are bigger than the mistakes. This is your true point of power. Describe a time when you failed and how that circumstance has benefited you.

Remember who you are.

Think back to a time when you felt loved, confident, proud of yourself, accepted, valued, connected--any or all of these things will do. Close your eyes and focus with full attention on what that felt like. Let it warm your soul and lift your spirits. That is the real you. The authentic you. The best version of you. Now face the day as that you. Your outer circumstances cannot trump who you are inside and what you bring to the world.

The longer you insist on identifying with what you don't have, the harder it becomes to recognize what you do have.

We humans have an innate tendency to focus on what is missing and lacking. We are drawn towards the deficit even in the face of some pretty incredible assets. In reality, our worlds generally contain generous portions of both negative and positive but our gravitation towards the negative can leave us living in a skewed representation of all that is present with us.

In the space below, make a list of 5 situations or circumstances which you perceive as negative or that represent a lack to you. Now go back and at the end of each item, write "&". Next to the "&" write down something that exists with you now that is an asset, a plus, a benefit, something you are genuinely thankful for. Recognize your power to choose which you will focus on all throughout the day.

Focus your fire.

Pick one thing today and give it all you've got. Focus your power and energy there with a no holds barred mentality. Record your experience below.

You are a force to be reckoned with. Own that.

Feel the brilliance of your shine and see your radiance flow from you, catching fire all around you. This is who you are. Go be that.

Never apologize for your brilliance. Don't be afraid to shine. The only thing that happens when you dim your light to suit the comfort of those around you is the whole world gets a little darker.

Where will you focus your light today?

Be kind to you. You more than anyone know exactly what it is you need to feel loved, safe, and cared for. Practice being there for yourself.

The art of self-care is greatly neglected and yet critical to our well being. What things are you doing to care for yourself? Write about them and what need they fill below.

If the answer is none, use the space below to write down three things you will do this week to care for you. Consider this a sacred promise to care for your mind, body, and spirit and return to this space to record your experiences.

You are the most influential person in your life. Speak to yourself with all the love and tenderness you can muster. Always.

If our inner chatter were suddenly to be broadcast aloud to the world around us, most of us would be horrified at the things we say to ourselves. Today catch any harsh inner chatter and then say to yourself: "Those words and that tone are how I used to communicate with myself. I have a better way of speaking to myself now. Today I choose to practice being kind, compassionate and loving in my inner chatter. I will continue to practice this way of speaking to myself until it becomes a habit." Then replace the harsh words with a statement that reflects tenderness and compassion. Write some words of encouragement in the space below.

Do not allow broken circumstances to convince you that you are broken. You are not broken. You are strong and you are right where you're supposed to be to realize just how strong.

Sometimes uncomfortable situations come to remind us how capable we are. Write down three ways you have demonstrated strength, resourcefulness, and capableness in the past.

Few changes take place in giant leaps. Most happen one tiny improvement at a time. Cherish every victory, no matter how small.

Celebrate a small victory today, even if it occurred weeks or months ago. Choose to cherish it today. Write about it below.

May your fear of not trying always be greater than your fear of failing and your willingness to be brave always stronger than the comfort of playing it safe.

If you had to name your adventure as you journey through life, what would you call it? Write it down below. Does the name give you power, or take power from you? Does it reflect your beauty, your brilliance, your value?

The appearance of difficulty only serves as notice that we are meant to, and able to, achieve far more than we have imagined we could.

No one likes seasons of hardship. Yet they usher in opportunities like no other for us to expand our understanding of who we are and of how capable and resourceful and resilient we are. Take a few minutes to reflect on what current difficulties are teaching you about who you are. Explore the person you are becoming in the process and lean into an understanding that this too will work for your good.

The Korean word "han" denotes a feeling of great sadness with hope. I love the thought of giving ourselves permission to feel both emotions with neither one crowding out the other. Labeling what we are feeling, honoring where we are, is a powerful choice.

List some seemingly contradictory emotions that you are feeling today. Allow yourself to fully settle into acknowledging all emotions without judging. Create a safe space where no emotion is ignored in preference of another. Reflect on your ability to acknowledge their presence without feeling pressured to choose one or the other but to simply be with what is.

Today your spirit is free to drink in beauty, revel in kindness, savor silence, and join in laughter. This is your day, it belongs to you. It is your space in time to experience as only you can. Fill it with things that bring you joy.

What are some things that bring you joy? How can you bring more of those experiences into the moments that fill your days?

The true test of strength is found in the ability to be gentle. The world needs more kindness, less judging. More humility, less posturing.

Make the conscious choice to be gentle today. Notice the feeling of power that comes when you choose a gentle response. Write about your experience below.

My beauty is not defined by what the mirror reflects back to me but by who I choose to be when the world is ugly around me.

Write about a time you had to consciously choose to be beautiful in the midst of ugly circumstances.

Insist on remaining attentive to the presence of those miracles which wear the camouflage of the everyday landscape of your life.

List five things that you take for granted which greatly enhance your life. Consider how much different your life would be if those things were not present. Share this new awareness with a friend.

Never allow your wounds to speak louder than your desire to heal.

What step can you take towards healing today? Be specific.

A better tomorrow begins with asserting hope today that a better tomorrow is possible. It is our nature to dream, to hope, to overcome.

Humans dream by default. We naturally strain towards what is larger than our current situation. We navigate toward what is better, though unknown, inspired by visions that arise from within our imaginations. What are your dreams saying to you today about your tomorrow?

You can be defined by your circumstances or by how you rise above them. The role of victim or champion is cemented within that choice.

Recall a situation where you have felt like a victim. Examine that situation for signs of your power, for clues to your ability to overcome and triumph in that circumstance. Look for evidence of you as a champion navigating that situation and coming out on top. Write about your discoveries below.

The darkness may roar, it may threaten, it may beckon, but it cannot consume you without your permission.

When the darkness threatens to overcome us, we have the power to refuse it permission. Where do you need to assert your authority over the darkness today? What would that look like?

Each day presents opportunities to choose love over hate, grace over judgment, and action over lethargy. We are the sum total of these choices.

List some good choices you have made this past week. Be specific. Notice how it feels to acknowledge your good choices.

Holding hope is not enough. You must act on that hope and align your thoughts with it til there is no room for anything else than that hope.

What two things can you do today to align your actions with your hopes? Write down how you plan to do that.

Falling down is part of the human experience. It's when you dare to get back up that things really begin to get interesting.

Write about an experience where you failed and fell short. Have you decided to get back up? If so, how has getting back up added to your story? If not, how can you get back up today?

Be about people, not agendas, people. Speak to the potential in them and move in favor of who they can be.

List one specific thing you can do to today to affirm the potential in someone who has been placed within your influence.

If what you're after isn't worth sacrificing for, it's probably not worth having.

What sacrifices have you had to make thus far? Did they surprise you? How have your sacrifices helped you solidify your commitment to reaching your goal? What have you learned from those experiences that can help you the next time a sacrifice is required of you?

Gratitude is a way of life, thankfulness a choice. Not because the good always outweighs the bad, but because it's what we choose to focus on.

Focus on what is right today. Just for today, make it a point to notice and to note, all that is right. Capture some of those things by writing about them below.

It's not about eliminating fear, it's about beating it. Its presence need not deter us from moving forward, nor sway us from our goal.

You may be terrified, but that does not mean you can't move towards your goal anyway. What step can you take today, however small, even while feeling afraid? Write about it below.

Until you shed your identity with those things you see as limiting you, you will remain confined to their version of who you can be.

Write down three things you believe are preventing you from being who you want to be. Now decide, are you willing to surrender your future, your identity, your destiny to those three things? Write your answer below.

Success is not the art of not getting knocked down but a consequence of refusing to stay down.

Encourage someone today who has experienced a setback. Let them know you believe they have what it takes to get back up and you are there to walk beside them.

We believe the reality we perceive and perceive the reality we believe. It's our insistence that things are so that makes them so.

If there were one thing, one situation, you could take a different and empowering perspective on, what would that be? Decide now to assert your power to choose how you will view that situation. Write how that new perspective will serve you and your dream.

However far-fetched or unlikely, put your dreams into words. Etch them on paper, in thought, and on tongue. Dare to call them forth.

Write down your dream in the present tense as though it were reality occurring now. Read it aloud each day for a full month. Be open to taking steps towards that dream each and every day.

We are defined by neither our successes nor our failures but by how and who we love.

Practice wholehearted love today. The kind of love that does not require someone to change in order to receive it and which has no expectations of reward. Love for the pure sake of loving. Give this love first to yourself, then to others. How else can you share love, except by first receiving it to give away?

Always be larger than the space you are in. Dream bigger, think bigger, act bigger than the confines and circumstances of the present moment.

How can you act bigger than your circumstances today?

What chases us from our sleep and robs us of our slumber is not the fear of failure but of being perceived as a failure.

Today, make it a point to NOT be concerned with how others perceive you. Give their reactions, judgments, and assessments no thought. Instead, devote all energy to simply being the best version of you and loving what you see.

I used to pray for miracles to appear. Now I pray for eyes to see the thousands of miracles present with me each and every day.

What are some miracles present with you this minute that you have overlooked?

Purpose often develops in the presence of blinding pain. Your deepest wounds may very well one day be the source of your greatest strength.

History bears testament to some of life's greatest tragedies giving birth to some of life's greatest acts of charity and love. What purpose can you lay hold of today which has its roots in pain?

In the space between our dreams and what we, in reality, will do to attain them resides the origins of both success and failure.

What is required of you to achieve the goal you are after? Are you willing to walk that out? Who might you turn to for support and encouragement along the way?

Immeasurable harm is wrought the moment we agree to be defined by who we are not and by what we have not.

Humans are hardwired to notice what is missing or lacking. We scan constantly, comparing ourselves and our circumstances to those around us. This is a death sentence to wholehearted living. Today write down 10 things that you are and celebrate them. Follow up with writing down 10 things you do have and give genuine thanks for them, noticing how they enrich your life.

I believe we all have the capacity to create something beautiful.

What is your "art"? How does it make you feel to create it? How can you add more of it to your life starting today?

Wishing doesn't produce change. Movement produces change. How ever small a step it may seem in comparison to your goal, keep moving forward.

What one, small, meaningful step can you take today to keep moving forward?

Without the willingness to embrace what is inconvenient it is impossible to become the person you are capable of being.

Write about an inconvenience you are experiencing that is necessary for your journey. Assure yourself, this too will pass. Give yourself permission to master this inconvenience and be ready and willing to share with others on their journey.

Don't ever allow a closed door to define the possibilities of your future. Keep walkin', keep talkin', keep knockin' til you find a way in.

How can you take specific action today to find a way in?

The only thing you can know for certain you can control is the way you respond to the circumstances that introduce themselves to you.

When difficulties present themselves to you, how do you introduce yourself to them? Are you their worst nightmare or a timid pushover? Take the space below to write out an introduction to a current hardship you are facing.

Be grateful for the moment that you're in. Whatever it looks like, however it arrived, it belongs to you and you alone. Make the most of it.

What positive quality can you find in the current moment to immerse yourself in? What sense of wonder and gratitude can be found within your current circumstances? Detail them below.

Fear is part and parcel of leaving your comfort zone. Make up your mind that it may be along for the ride but it will never steer the wheel.

Name five things you are afraid of. Acknowledge that everyone feels afraid. Now acknowledge you have the power to choose to disregard the chatter of fear and press on anyway. Name one specific item you will do today even though you feel afraid.

When the answers we have are woefully inadequate for the questions posed, hope must come not from a place of understanding but of trusting.

What situation must you offer up trust for today? What does that mean to you? How can you affirm your trust? What words do you need to say? What prayer do you need to pray to solidify your commitment to trust? Write your remarks below.

Stand your ground as others scatter, press on when others step away, set aside what's been for what can be and you will achieve what others only dream.

Are there people you thought would make the journey with you who have left you to travel on alone? Write their names below. Now speak words of blessing and peace over them. Release them to their journey and give thanks for the time you shared. Know you are capable and able to make the journey without them. If they were meant to make the journey with you, they would be.

Freedom begins with the thought that you can be free.

What does freedom mean for you? How does it feel, smell, taste?
Write in great detail below.

It's not an obstacle, it's an opportunity to sharpen your skills and discover new giftings. This is to grow you, not to slow you.

We don't have to be thrilled when we come face to face with yet another setback. However, if we don't recognize there is value within the adversity we miss the point. Even if begrudgingly, care enough about your journey to seek for the gift within the obstacle.

Reflect on a current hardship and write what possible gifts it might contain.

At some point being who you need to be will clash with who others say you need to be. Have the courage to stand your ground. Your future self is counting on it.

You need no one's permission to be who it is you were created to be. Write a promise to your future self below, to be true to the authentic you, to support, love, and cherish your uniqueness, and to seek out circumstances and people who affirm your right to be you.

Make a plan but be willing to adapt to what develops along the way. What seems like a detour may be the path you've needed all along.

Is there an area of your life you've been insisting must be a certain way but inside you know you need to let go and take the detour? Write about it below. Affirm your trust in your instincts and express a willingness to be led in the right direction. Congratulate yourself on this step in your journey.

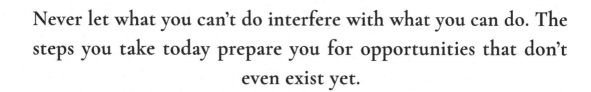

Never let what you can't do interfere with what you can do. The steps you take today prepare you for opportunities that don't even exist yet.

Have you been underestimating the power of what you can do right here right now? What can you do today? Be specific.

Don't forget to remember who you are through all of the shifting and changing of seasons, settings, and surrounding cast members of your life.

Cultivate a trust in who you are. The voice of approval you most need to hear is your own. What can you say to yourself right here, right now, that will be of help to you? Write it below.

Failing doesn't keep you from succeeding. Not trying keeps you from succeeding.

What are some excuses you use to justify not trying? List them below. Are you willing to give them up? Which ones? What action can you take to demonstrate your willingness to abandon them?

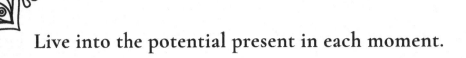

Live into the potential present in each moment.

Each moment contains the potential for joy, for sorrow, for wonder, for thankfulness, for judgment, for grace. All throughout this day be mindful and intentional with the potential you seize from each moment. Write about your experiences below.

If you will set aside what you can't do and give all you are to what you can do, you, my friend, will accomplish remarkable things.

What percentage of your time and mental energy would you estimate you devote to thoughts of what you can't do? To what you can do? What does your answer say about the direction you are heading?

One of the few things in life we can control are the words that come out of our mouths. Speak hope, speak life, speak love. Always.

Choose three people today and make an intentional choice to speak words of life to them. In the space below, write their names. After your interaction with them, return here and write the date of when you spoke with them. Trust those words will take root and continue to bear fruit.

Show me where you're broken and I'll show you a place where it's possible to heal and be stronger than you were before.

Offer your broken places in complete trust, knowing there is healing for even the deepest of your wounds. Allow this knowledge to soothe your sorrows and comfort your spirit. Affirm below that you are already healing. Express gratitude for the strength that is flowing within you. Know that all is well.

We are shaped by our choices of what we direct our time, energy, and thoughts towards.

Write down the major categories of your life. Today keep a journal of where you devote your time, thoughts, and energy. Is there a need for any adjustments? What might those adjustments be?

Your future self doesn't need you to not fail. Your future self needs you to know what to do with your failures.

It is no secret that the greatest successes stand on the shoulders of great failures. The ability to know what to do after having failed is critical to reaching success. Where and whom have you failed and how can you begin today to make amends? List specific steps you can take today in the space below.

It's an obstacle, not an excuse. Something to overcome, not a reason to run from what you know you came here to do.

List the obstacles currently in your way. Are you willing to allow them to have the final say on how your story ends? Write your answer below.

Some burdens can be carried for so long that we see them as part of who we are and forget we have the ability to choose to lay them down.

What is heavy within you? What burden, what situation, what circumstance have you allowed to become part of your identity? What can you do today to lay that aside? Recognize who you are has nothing to do with the experiences you've had. You always have been, and always will be, far greater than any one moment in time.

Wisdom is knowing when to stand and fight and when to walk away. Not every battle is worth fighting or even yours to fight.

Are there any battles in your life you are fighting that you should no longer be fighting? How did this come to be? How can you be free? Record your thoughts below.

The ability of fear to overwhelm us is not derived from the scenarios it proposes but from our willingness to accept them as truth.

Today, question your fears. All of them. Ask if they are absolutely 100% for certain the truth. Ask what other possible scenarios exist. Write your responses below.

If you're overwhelmed by the prospect of pushing back the covers to face the day, realize the instant you do so, you've won. Nothing else the whole day may go your way, but you have already won.

Courage comes in many forms. How are you showing courage today? Give yourself full credit for what it takes to live the life you are living.

Get knocked down-Get back up. As long as you understand it's a two part process, you will always come out a winner.

Why do you think we tend to focus on the part where we fell down, instead of looking for ways to get back up? How can looking at failure as a two part redemptive process help you in your current circumstances?

Let life's random imperfections remind you perfection is not necessary to live fully here and now.

Have you ever been forced to go ahead with something when it wasn't the ideal time or setting for it and found it turned out just fine anyway? We often use the excuse of waiting for the perfect time, connection, resource, (fill in the blank) as a stall tactic because we've convinced ourselves nothing less than perfect will do. Which simply isn't true.

Name a circumstance that you know you need to move forward with in the space below. Commit to setting aside your desire for perfection and instead, take the next logical step towards your goal. Return to this space to write about the outcome.

The battles hardest fought strip us of our complacency and push us to a place where we can no longer comfortably sit idly by.

Adversity can light a fire under us by forcing us to get real about how badly we want something. Recall a time when you knew for certain you could no longer settle for things the way they were. Write about that experience below.

People who change the world focus on what they can bring to an environment rather than on what they can get from it.

Today in every interaction, focus on what you are bringing to the situation and the environment, rather than on what you can get from it. Record your experiences below.

One of the most difficult things to do is to keep going when it doesn't seem to be making a difference. It does and you can.

We know we can't see it all. We understand things are happening even though out of our sight but it's difficult not to be discouraged when there are no measurable results.

Today, measure your efforts, not the results. Give yourself credit for the good choices you make and find satisfaction in giving your best self. In the space below journal about the steps you took today and the efforts you gave. See them through the eyes of someone outside the situation to help you key in on all that you accomplished today and acknowledge your courage.

The words that you speak, the air that you breathe, are one and the same. Your words create your environment.

What are your power words? The words that inspire you and ignite your desire for greatness? Record them below and find a way to introduce them into your world all throughout this day.

You were created with significance, here on purpose for a purpose, and you are just who you need to be to fulfill that purpose.

What is your purpose? What feelings does your purpose evoke within you? What steps can you take today to walk confidently in that purpose?

It's only a problem if you say it's a problem. Otherwise, it's a solution in progress.

This single shift in thinking moves us from stuck to limitless possibilities. What solutions are in progress in your life today?

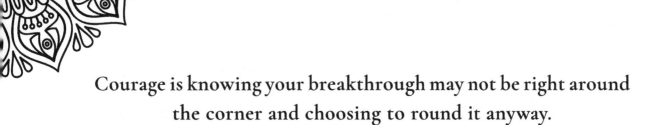

Courage is knowing your breakthrough may not be right around the corner and choosing to round it anyway.

Name someone who is now successful who had a long and difficult journey? How can their journey inspire you? What step are you willing to take today with no guarantee of success? Do you see that as being courageous? How can the practice of putting yourself out there benefit you long term? Write your thoughts below.

You cannot be too broken to be whole again, nor so lost you cannot be found. No matter where you are, you are not alone. His love heals all.

We tend to think that other people can get better, but our wounds are too deep, the situation too intense. We see an asterisk beside every promise of hope, love, and healing that says *Except for me. This kind of thinking keeps us living far below our potential and in continual pain, hiding our true selves. Our wounds don't disqualify us from the Creator's love, they are precisely the reason He came and gave His love. How can knowing this, change the way you view your woundedness?

The night pretends authority it does not possess and lays claim to territory it cannot own. Its deception is revealed as it kneels to the dawn.

Recall a time when you thought the night had won, but dawn did indeed return. How did you feel to know the darkness had ended? What did you learn from that experience? Be specific.

Our tendency to offer acceptance only to those who look, think, and act as we look, think, and act deprives us of countless opportunities for true connection and intimacy. When we are secure in who we are, we are not threatened by who others are, and within the space that acceptance creates, wonderful things can happen.

Today give someone a safe space to be completely who they are. Offer love and acceptance of them without advice on how they can be different or do better. Give them a judgment free zone to just be. You don't have to like what they've done or agree with their current beliefs to offer acceptance in acknowledgment of the humanity common between you.

Someone failing to recognize your worth is not a statement of your worth but rather of their inability to see and comprehend it.

Are there people in your life that are incapable of seeing your value? How do you deal with those people? What boundaries do you have in place to protect you from their toxicity?

When the fear of not trying exceeds the fear of failing, and when risking what is pales in comparison to losing what could be, you are ready to win.

When was the first time you remember realizing you were more afraid of not trying than of failing? How has that changed your outlook and your behaviors?

Do not judge your path by the path of another. Comparison only serves as a distraction from the destiny you were brought here to fulfill.

You are right where you are supposed to be doing exactly what you are supposed to be doing. It's not too late or too soon and you are not too old, too uneducated, too poor. You are just enough of you. Get back to the dream within you. You are it's keeper. It's presence within you the proof you are meant to fulfill it. Write about your dream below and how excited you are that it is YOUR dream.

You belong even when others reject you. You are worthy of love even when others judge you unacceptable. You are worthwhile even when others find you lacking. Their opinion of you is just that—their opinion.

Take a few minutes and look up any current movie, book, or product. Focus on the reviews. Notice how different and varied they are. What is the greatest thing for one person is deemed completely unacceptable by another. In the end, if you were to go see that movie, read that book, or purchase that product, your opinion would carry much more weight than any you have read. Today, make it a point to not be swayed by the opinions of those around you regarding your capableness, worthiness, and value. Let your voice and your opinion be the only one that matters in your world.

Vulnerability is a prerequisite for success of any kind. You've got to be willing to look foolish and be okay with getting a little messed up in the process of becoming your best self.

Your best self is not perfect, but it is enough. It takes courage to be vulnerable (imperfect) in a world obsessed with perfection. Who are the people in your life you know love you just the way that you are? How has their love and acceptance been an asset to you? How can you show that kind of love and acceptance to others?

Pain is part of healing. Ignore it and it festers, wallow in it and you will drown. Face it honestly and restoration is already on the way.

Loving yourself means letting go of old wounds and relinquishing their power in your life. Are there areas of pain that need to be healed in your life? List one step you could take today towards healing. Write your answer below. Hold yourself accountable to take this step, knowing it is ushering in a more wholehearted way of living.

Our deepest wounds arise not from the actions of others but from the meaning, power, and influence we assign to those actions.

Consider any grudges you may be holding onto. We often believe they have a hold on us, but in reality, it is us holding onto them. Those areas of resentment stunt our growth and keep us living small.

As unlikely as it may seem, you need you to forgive that person more than they need you to forgive them. Name the person(s) below that you need to forgive. Start by writing a letter to them. You may never feel comfortable giving the letter to them and that is okay. Your power is in choosing to forgive. The act of forgiveness does not justify what happened, it doesn't absolve them from responsibility, but it does free you of its power and the pain it left behind.

Boldly live who you are and who you aren't will cease to matter.

Name three absolutely amazing qualities about you and write about how you are able to use those qualities to increase joy and satisfaction in your life.

Feed your insecurities and they will grow until they become the hindrance you've believed they are.

Most of us have a huge list of all the things we wish we were better at or more of. More often than not our attention is focused on all the ways we believe we are not good enough and we actually look for proof that this is true in our daily lives.

Write down three things you are insecure about and for the next seven days, search for proof that the opposite is true. Return to the space below to record your findings.

There's a place in each of us where dreams persist, hope remains, and strength is renewed. A place deep within where we know we are enough.

We all know the sensation of being in perfect alignment with our true self. That magical moment where we know we are loved, know we are safe, know we are bringing our best self to the world and making a difference. Those moments where all seems right within and without and joy comes effortlessly.

Write about a time when you felt you were in perfect rhythm with all of life. What circumstances, thoughts, and activities were you engaged in? Examine what you were doing, the choices you were making, the energies you were focused on. Use this knowledge to increase those magical moments of synchronicity. They are clues to who you are meant to be.

You cannot become the person you dream of being until you fully appreciate the person you already are.

We are so good at seeing what we aren't good at that it takes work to pinpoint and focus on those things we do well. In the space provided write down three things you do really well, no matter how insignificant or unimportant they may seem. Realize that somewhere, someone is wishing they could do those things well. They are a gift, your gift, to the world around you. They, and you, are worth celebrating.

So maybe, just maybe, whatever wasn't or isn't what you wanted showed up not to limit what could be but to motivate you to soar far above all limitations.

Is there a circumstance in your life that feels like it could crush you? Stop to imagine for just a few minutes that you discover you are able to rise above it with little difficulty. That just the right perspective, resources, power, energy, and help is delivered just in time for you to soar above it. What would that feel like? What sorts of thoughts might be running through your mind at that time? To whom and for what might you be grateful?

Our broken places can spur us to deeper compassion, cement purpose within us, or cripple us where we stand. Always the choice is ours.

Is there a circumstance in your life that has caused you to have greater compassion and empathy towards others? Write about it below.

If all of the things you have in your life to be grateful for could somehow be gathered together in one place, would you recognize them?

What are some of the things in your life that you have taken for granted again and again? List them below and pause to consider the value they bring to your world.

We act in ways consistent with what we believe. If you're stuck, examine your beliefs. Adjust them and consistently act on those new beliefs.

Are you stuck today? What beliefs are supporting you being stuck? How can you adjust those beliefs so that they serve you rather than hinder you?

Perseverance is not accidental but a choice to remain true to the goal before you no matter what lies in the space between here and there.

Write about a time you have persevered. How can that experience help you in your current reality?

If you have learned to worry, then you can learn to trust. If you have learned to fear, then you can learn to be at peace.

Today begin an education in how to trust. Gather around you what you need to know to be at peace. Pursue this knowledge and understanding. Seek outside help, search deep within, do not take this pursuit lightly. Write about your experiences below and return to this space to record new thoughts along the way.

The decision to continue when no one would notice if we quit is one of the most difficult battles to fight and the one most necessary to win.

Take note of the times you feel strong and capable. Store those memories faithfully. Write down the joys of triumph. Return to those places in time anytime you feel discouragement settling in. Build up a bank of powerful success memories to stay you through the seasons of doubt. Write some memories of success below and ponder them throughout this day.

Finding a place of peace, of belief in all things working together for your good, is a choice. It's not imposed upon you, it is chosen.

Name a concrete way you can choose peace today.

You will encounter imperfection today, less than ideal situations, and perhaps even disappointment. You will encounter people who are unkind, judgmental, rude and self-absorbed. Do not allow any of that to distract you from all that is good and right and beautiful in this world.

Take a few minutes now to list five things that are present in your life that truly bring you joy, or comfort, or a sense of satisfaction. Focus on those things in your life that are of beauty, of worth, and of significance. Allow gratitude for their presence to saturate your thoughts and linger there a while. Realize though these things may not have the power to take away the hardships, difficulties, and ugly places of life, you have the power to center your thoughts, your focus, and your attention on them.

All beings are worthy of being treated with dignity, kindness, and compassion. Including the one who stares back at you in the mirror each morning.

We demand that those in positions of great power take care great care to treat those over whom they have power with dignity, fairness, and compassion. We recognize their influence affords them considerable impact on those within their reach. We insist that those who wield power do no harm, yet we often use our own power to inflict great pain upon ourselves.

No one has more influence over your physical, emotional, and spiritual well being than you do. Therefore, it is to your own self that you have the greatest responsibility to be gentle, and kind, and loving. What can you do today to begin giving yourself the benefit of your most generous encouragement and most sincere and non-judgmental compassion? Write your thoughts in the space below.

Powerlessness begins the moment we grant a situation authority over who we can be and what we can achieve.

In the space below write a decree of emancipation from any situation that has limited you. Take your power back as you write those words. Know that you exist far outside the confines of any experience and you have the power to choose to be who it is you want to be.

Gratitude isn't something that just happens. It's a mindset that is achieved through mindful attention to and appreciation of the many wonderful things that wear the camouflage of ordinary conveniences and quiet blessings.

Explore the last hour of your life. Search it for five things which are not necessarily incredibly spectacular but which enrich your life in subtle and gentle ways. Write about them in the space below.

Get around people who inspire you, people who ignite your passion for your dreams, people in whose presence your impossible seems possible.

Name some of your heroes, fictional or literal. What about their stories inspires you? What can you take from what they've accomplished to help you in your journey? Every now and then when you're doubting yourself, have a conversation with them--even if only in your head. Let their strength and courage and resolve be contagious. They persevered and found success and so can you.

Any worthwhile pursuit will call you to stretch further than you believe you can. First, we shape the dream, then the dream shapes us.

Write about some of the ways the dream is shaping you. Are there any surprises in this new awareness?

The secret of those who do the impossible is that they believe they can and act in accordance with that belief.

What one action can you take today that aligns you with what you say you believe about your purpose?

Those content to offer commentary on how a warrior has fallen reveal their own wounds in the decision to inject criticism rather than grace.

Reach out with grace today rather than with a criticism or judgment. Write about a time when you needed that and what it felt like to receive grace in that place.

So you've got stuff. We've all got "stuff". Everybody falls, everybody fails. Question is are you going to let that be the end of your story?

See your current circumstances as just a chapter in your story. How would you like this chapter to end? What are you hoping to gain from this chapter? What plans are you making for next chapter? Write about it below.

You don't have to get right back up but the longer you lie there, the more identified you become with the fall. You are so much more.

Falling down can hurt. A lot. It's tempting to stay put and wallow in our disappointment. What words do you most need to hear to see the fall as a temporary setback and not as your identity? Write them below. Practice using them any time you are tempted to stay down.

The world is full of people who are committed to running the race. Be the kind of person who is committed to finishing the race.

What does your finish line look like? Who will be there? What kind of person will you be then? What will your priorities be? How will you acknowledge you are at the finish line? Write your responses below.

The environments and relationships you place yourself in wield a power like no other. You become what you give yourself to, choose well.

Look over your relationships. Are there some that drag you down and away from your true purpose? What steps can you take today to disconnect yourself from them? What healthy relationships can you invest more into? What would those investments look like? Write your thoughts in the space below.

When surrounded by darkness, speak life, speak hope, speak better days to come. The night will fall away as it always does. You, your purpose, and your place, will remain.

Find a quiet place, write a letter of encouragement to yourself. Acknowledge all you've been through. Acknowledge how far you've come. Admit your resourcefulness, your strength, your creativity. Predict the best is yet to come and assure yourself you will take note of and cherish every win along the way. Paint a picture of what the final outcome will be and celebrate the steps already taken towards this end.

No reasoning nor argument will ever render fear as powerless as simply moving towards what you want in spite of it. You move, you win.

MOVE today. MOVE towards your goal. MOVE towards health. MOVE towards intimacy. MOVE in spite of the fear. Write the ways you move today in the space below.

If there were no battles to fight, no races to run, nor mountains to climb, how would you know you're a champion?

Take stock today of the many ways you've become acquainted with yourself through what seemed tedious, difficult, or inconvenient. Write your thoughts below.

Never discount the power of small but positive changes as they are the seeds of revolution and transformation. Once sown the landscape cannot remain the same.

What small positive change can you make today? What are you hoping this small change will grow to be? How can you tend to this seed? Write about it in the space below.

Grief reminds us we have places, people, and experiences of value. It reveals what we hold as precious, gives testament to what we treasure.

Grief is a sacred acknowledgment of joys and loves we've known. Write about some of the moments of grief you've experienced and what they taught you to treasure and appreciate. Give thanks for the presence of those memories and allow them to speak to you.

The night ceases reign the moment we decide we will not succumb to it, will not bow down, will not lie down, but will stand tall however long.

What has facing the night taught you about standing tall?
Write your thoughts below.

Let your words reflect the highest of regard for the brilliant and Divine creation that you are. Practice being on your own side. Argue for the future you want to see and in favor of the person you came here to be.

Listen to how you talk about your future. What future are you arguing for? Are you arguing in favor of your success? Are you adamant in coming to your own defense? Write down your thoughts below.

Before the triumph of the finish line, there are miles to be traveled without cheering crowds. Persist in the silence and you will see the victory won.

What strengths of yours might be cultivated in the times of silence? How can being quiet help you today?

There are often periods of time and space between the questions and the answers. You must fill them with trust or the questions will pull you under.

What would filling the time and space with trust mean for you? How can you begin to do this today? What are some of the questions you need answers for? How can you demonstrate trust right here right now? Record your thoughts below.

LIFE IS HARD

Too often we leap to point out where someone has fallen instead of reaching down to help them up, forgetting our own desperate need of grace.

Help someone up today, this week, this month. Make it a regular part of who you are. Return to this space to write about your experiences.

The night may persist but it cannot take away our choice to battle on in spite of it. Fight the good fight even when it's not convenient.

What is not convenient about your fight right now? Who or what can you turn to for help, support, and encouragement? What do you see the rewards of fighting through the inconvenience to be?

You can argue the walls around you are there to confine you or you can argue you are there to have a front row seat to see them crumble down.

What walls would you love to see come crumbling down? What will you do with your newfound freedom? Be specific.

Lies offered your faith become your truth. They wield the power to crush your spirit under the weight of the illusion of their authority.

What lies have you offered your faith to? Be specific. How has this impacted your life? What is the truth about these situations? Write them out in great detail. How can giving your faith to the truth set you free? Think of a way you can remind yourself daily of this new truth as you grow into it completely.

It's never about the mountain in our way, but what we believe about the mountain. Barrier, detour, or opportunity to attain new heights?

Pick any obstacle you are facing. Think of three ways this obstacle can benefit you and write your thoughts below.

Take heart! This day could be THE day your breakthrough arrives, the tide turns in your favor, the impossible becomes possible. STAND STRONG.

What does standing strong mean to you? Who do you have to stand by you while you stand strong? Reach out to them right now and let them know how much they mean to you.

It's okay to be who you are, where you are. Really.

Absorb this. Write it down below, inserting your own name. Now say it aloud. Now find a mirror or use the camera on your phone and throw your shoulders back, raise your head high, look yourself square in the eyes, and speak it aloud again. Using your phone record your voice speaking this aloud with great confidence. Play this anytime you need a reminder.

Make friends with the obstacles in your path. They are your greatest teachers.

Name something you have learned from facing an obstacle in your life. How can what you have learned help you today?

Your power to create a life worth living begins with understanding it is you who must choose to live it.

What are you waiting for? Be specific. What is holding you back? Are you waiting for someone else's approval? How can you begin today to claim your space, your power, your right to live your life?

Perfection demands a price that is never fully paid, promises love but yields only shame.

What are some of the promises perfection has made to you? Things you believe being perfect will provide for you or do for you? Be specific. Are you perfect? Will you ever be perfect? Name one way you can love your imperfect self today.

Go as far as you can possibly go—and then go one step more. Breakthroughs occur at the point we most feel like settling for good enough.

What does going one step more mean in relation to what you are currently experiencing in your life? What inspires you to keep going? Write about it below.

If we saw ourselves as capable of what God sees us as capable of, obstacles in our way would look less like obstacles and more like trophies.

What are some obstacles, I mean trophies, that you are currently collecting?

Many yearn to be remarkable, to stand out from the crowd, yet are unwilling to risk the vulnerability and exposure required to leave the pack.

Leaving the protection of the pack is terrifying and also completely necessary to live the life we are meant to live. Thank the pack for the lessons it has taught you and write out your words of thanks below. Know you have what it takes to venture out on your own now. Trust you will be provided with new teachers every step along the way and that each new level will bring new helpers.

Whether for or against, other's opinions of you remain only and exactly that. They must never be considered proof for or justification of your worth.

What are some of the nicest things that have ever been said about you? What are some of the most terrible things that have ever been said about you? What do you say about you?

Don't wait until you have it all together to begin living as the person you know you are capable of being.

Thinking of the qualities your ideal self would have, which of those could you summon forth today? How will this quality of your ideal self be put to use in your life today? Is there any reason not to actively use this quality today? Write your thoughts below.

Hope gives us permission to imagine an alternate ending. Faith is willing to bet on that ending becoming a reality.

Think of an alternate ending you are pulling for and write out the details below. Now decide on one thing you can do today to demonstrate your faith that this alternate reality is possible and go do that.

One of the strongest predictors of both success and failure is found in how a person responds to setbacks and disappointments.

How do you handle disappointments and setbacks? Do you see room for adjustment? What one shift would greatly benefit you? Write about it in the space below.

Worry is not the absence of faith, it is the application of our faith to the absolute worst possible outcome. What we give our faith to, we give life to.

What are you giving your faith to? Be honest.

Warrior, your pain need not define you nor your wounds bind you to circumstances now long past. Your power lies in your choices now.

What do you choose to do this day with your past wounds?

The biggest lie is that you can't. Can't win, can't succeed, can't be loved, can't do exactly what it is you came here to do. You can, you will, and you are. This, all of this, is part of the process.

What do you constantly feel you can't do? When those feelings of inadequacy arise, can you acknowledge they are just part of the process of growth? Then can you choose a different perspective? Such as "I am in the process of learning to _____. What I know today will be added to what I learn tomorrow and eventually, I will _____ ." In the space below write out the above sentences but fill in the blanks with the areas of your specific challenges.

The longer the battle, the more significant the victory. Don't lose heart—every day you persevere brings victory one day closer.

How are you refreshing your spirit along the way? Write out three things you can do to care for your soul. Pick one and do it today.

Maybe you can't see yourself achieving your dream, but can you see yourself taking just one small step towards it? Do that, repeat often.

What does one small step look like? How will you do it? What will you look like doing it? Write out your answers below. Decide to take that small step today.

Obstacles and setbacks often introduce us to a wiser, stronger, more resourceful version of ourselves than we'd previously believed could be.

Think about a time when a negative situation brought out the best in you or in someone you know. Write about it below. Give thanks for the opportunity to get in touch with these particular strengths.

More than any other words you will hear today, your internal chatter has the power to direct you towards success or failure.

What do you most need to hear from your own voice today? Write it out below and then speak it aloud.

Within the fabric of every failure lies the threads necessary to weave success. Don't allow what didn't work to blind you to what did.

What is working in your life today? Write out at least five items. Explore them. Soak them in. Give thanks for them. Share them with a friend.

There will always be someone who has more, who's done more. Don't stop reaching, but don't ever take for granted all that is with you now.

Think of three experiences, people, or opportunities that you are intensely grateful for. Allow that feeling of gratitude to fill your heart and flood your thoughts. How wonderful it is that these things are a part of your life's story! Give thanks for them in detail by writing in the space below.

Your circumstances can only speak as to your experiences, they cannot tell the story of who you are nor dictate who you will become.

Think of an experience that made you feel poorly. In the space below write out the facts of the experiences. Now write out the facts of who you are. See the difference? Tell your former self it's ok to shed his or her identity with this experience and that it is no longer allowed to speak for you.

Falling down does not equal defeat, staying down equals defeat. Champions are made in the decision to rise again and again to battle on.

Who do you have ringside urging you to get back up? Name them. Give thanks for them. Give thanks to them. Invest in those relationships often.

Whether it's joy or sorrow you are feeling, you are here now to feel it. You are here, and so there is hope and where there is hope, anything is possible.

Your presence here is not an accident and no matter what you are currently facing, the point is, you are here to feel it. Let the full impact of that statement soak in. What are some things you hope to do in your time here on this planet? List some of them below. Are there steps you can take today towards doing those things?

Your dreams give witness to the purpose you were created for. Don't abandon them, they are a forecast of who you can one day be.

What do your dreams say to you about who you are and the life you can live? How can you align your actions today with that vision?

The labels you allow become the limitations that you live, their confines your prison, their definitions your destiny.

Get some labels. They can be name tags, address labels, or packaging labels. Think about some of the labels you have allowed to speak for you. Write them each down on a label. Affix them to your body.

Who gave those particular labels to you? Where did they originate? How can you begin today to remove them and therefore their power over you? As you contemplate that, find a mirror and tear the labels one by one from your body symbolizing your refusal to wear those labels any longer. Place the labels into the space below and mark an X through each one. Know you are no longer bound by those definitions.

It's not what you have but what you're willing to give that defines your wealth.

List some things you are willing to give today. Return to the space below to record your experiences.

It's not the cost of what you are giving up to attain your goal, but the cost of not obtaining your goal which should be considered most.

What are you hoping to gain from achieving your dream? What will you have lost if you give up that pursuit? Write your thoughts below.

There is no question you were created to succeed. The only question is whether or not you will settle for anything less.

What does it look like when you bring your very best self to the challenges of your life? How do you feel? How do others respond? How do you view yourself and your future in those moments? Write out the details below.

The stamina and strength needed to reach your destination arises from the consistent appreciation and celebration of where you presently are.

Focus in on three elements of your current setting, situation, and experiences that you are thoroughly pleased with. How does it feel to have those things in place? What have you done to bring those things about? Did others contribute to them being a part of your life? In how many different ways can you show appreciation for them and the efforts that brought them to you?

Few things in this life can cost you as much as the decision to live for the approval of others. The authentic you requires no permission.

As you go about living your life today, check in with yourself often and assess why you are doing and saying the things you are doing and saying. Are they things you authentically want to participate in? Are you engaging out of a fear of what others will think if you do not? Are you holding yourself back because you are afraid of being judged? Make note today of any activity you are involved in or shying away from because of a need for the approval of others. Return to this space to record your thoughts.

Those things standing between us and our dreams are given their fierceness, their depth, and their breadth by our imagination of them.

How are you embellishing the things that stand in your way? What drama are you adding to the situation? What assumptions are you claiming as truth? At their core, what can really be said about these obstacles? What is the truth about their power and their stature? About your ability to circumvent them or remove them altogether? Record your answers in the space below.

We are not promised the absence of difficulties but that we can overcome them. A champion's path is not one of ease but it is one of victory.

What is your first response when you encounter a setback? Is it helpful? If the answer is "no", take some time to devise a strategy for coping with disappointments and setbacks. List your ideas below. Make certain they are strategies that will serve you well. Practice them every chance you get. Return to this space to readjust them as needed.

For there to be victory, there must be a battle.

If your battle were made into a movie, who would play the part of
you? What would you tell them about how you made it through the
most difficult times? What qualities would you stress to them would be
important to display? Write your answers in the space below.

A big picture bird's eye view renders obstacles the size of stepping stones. Your perspective matters more than the size of what you are facing.

Think of a substantial difficulty you are facing right now. Now, imagine you have the ability to zoom out of that singular focus, like zooming out on the earth via a satellite image, and notice all of the other circumstances and situations that are present with that particular difficulty. Some of those circumstances you will perceive as negative, and some as positive. Now realize that you can choose at any time what to focus on and to what degree. Write your thoughts below.

Our capacity for change is limited only by the capacity of our imagination and our willingness to act on that which we can imagine.

What actions can you take on things you have so far only imagined?
Be specific. Write your thoughts below.

You can see the mountain as keeping you from where you want to go—or as a way to get a clear view of the best way to get there.

Elevate may seem like trite advice, but it has meaningful value when we genuinely decide to undertake that process. How would the you who is capable of climbing that mountain view the journey to the top of the mountain? As a problem or as an adventure? As a difficulty or as a thrill? Write your thoughts down below.

Love someone today simply because you can. No agenda, no thought to getting anything in return, purely for the sake of loving.

Have you ever been the recipient of unconditional love? Love with no pre-requisites, no judgment, no limitations? How did that impact your life? Write your thoughts below. If you've never experienced that kind of love, make a space in your heart for it now and begin by loving yourself just as you are.

Perseverance is never pretty, often lonely, and more than a few parts straight up insanity. It's being tough while remaining soft. It's learning to act big while feeling small. It's laying it all on the line because giving only part of you just won't do.

What motivates you to persist? How can you bring more of that inspiration into your life? Write your responses below.

Purpose is found not in getting but in giving—and everyone, EVERYONE, has something of value to give. When you get that, it changes everything.

What can you give today? Give specific details. Return to this space to write your experiences.

Never allow what you don't have to dictate the size of your dreams. Don't have it? Get it. Don't know it? Learn it.

Make a list of five things you believe you lack to reach your goal. Now list who it is or where it is you could find a connection to or a resource that could fill that void. Reach out today to at least one of those sources of possible solutions. Record your experiences below.

One of the most powerful gifts you could ever give someone is to let them know you see them as being more than their current situation.

We all need a little reminder from time to time that we are bigger than our problems. Today be intentional about reaching out with genuine encouragement to someone you know is struggling. Speak words of life to them and let them know you see them as capable of success.

To remain authentic in a world addicted to conformity requires the willingness to lose the approval of others in order to hold your own intact.

Have you lost the approval of others along the way? How did you handle it? Knowing what you know now, would you adjust anything? What would that be? Write your responses down below.

In chasing the illusion of how things should be we forfeit the greatness that can only come from abandoning the confines of the expected.

Set a timer for five minutes. Think of a situation that has been causing you stress. Now, imagine all of the possible outcomes for that situation. It doesn't matter how improbable or unlikely. Allow your imagination to run wild. Let the alternate endings unfold in your mind like a movie. Notice the color, the excitement, the intensity. How does it feel to have no limitations? Do the scenarios make you smile? Are they comical? Dramatic? What elements of who you are do you find in their unraveling? Are there certain needs you have that those imagined scenarios are picking up? Is there anything at all you can learn from what your imagination offers up? Write about your experience below.

The past can only speak to what was, the present only to what is. Neither has any authority over what is yet to be, save what you allow.

Come into the present moment by anchoring your gaze and drawing a deep breath. Allow your shoulders to relax. Notice the sights and colors around you. Imagine what this scene might look like five years from now. Notice how futile it is to try to predict that with any certainty. Decide to appreciate what is with you now and list three things you find of beauty, or interest, or which bring peace. Allow the power of the present moment to fill your thoughts.

Happiness is not a far off event arising from the external but is found in our choice to recognize the magnificence of the moment with us now.

The ability to evoke a sense of wonder is something every human being possesses. It is available to us at any time. Consider your current circumstances and find a place within which acknowledges the beauty of life. Immerse yourself in the wonder of you being here at this point in history to bear witness to it.

Sometimes we are meant to listen rather than to speak.

Practice listening today. Give someone the gift of your full attention today. Be mindful of your tendency to be absent from the conversation by worrying about what you will say in reply. Detach from the need of your ego to compose a response and instead fully connect to what they are saying. Notice how you feel in offering this space to them. When they are done speaking, let your words to them flow from the space of having fully heard their voice. Write about your experiences below.

Insecurities have a lot to say. None of it is in any way relevant to being the brilliant light that you are. You can choose to listen and play it small, or ignore their incessant chatter and shine like only you can.

Ever notice that our insecurities always seem to have the same thing to say? Much like a video stuck on a loop, they repeat the same thing over and over again. Recognize these are nothing more than internal alarms set off by your decision to go outside your comfort zone. They are part of the process of becoming your best self. Redirect your attention away from them by focusing on the fact that they have shown up because you are going after something awesome. Write about that awesome something in the space below.

The impossible only exists to dare us to dream beyond it, challenge us to rise above it, igniting the creativity needed to achieve it.

Name five things that were once thought to be impossible and list them below. Contemplate the courage it must have taken to insist these things could be in the face of public opinion and evidence to the contrary. Allow the courage and persistence of those dreamers to inspire you. Hold your dream in sacred regard and feed it your belief as often as you can.

Own your story but don't ever make the mistake of believing that it owns you. No circumstance can take away your ability to choose your response.

What are some of the major themes of your story? Do those themes serve you well? Do they reflect your power to heal, to chose, to be resilient, to be a champion? Are there some that need to be rewritten? Write your thoughts below.

Complaining is easy, mindless. Working towards a solution, that is an investment that stretches and develops body, mind, and spirit.

Count how many times you complain today. Each time you do, gently remind yourself of the opportunity to make an investment in a solution by giving up your right to gripe and working instead on finding a better way.

Write about your experiences here and how it feels to shift from placing blame to owning opportunity.

The choice to be brave does not relieve us of our fears but it does relieve them of their power over us.

Write about a time you were brave. Did you realize at the time that you were being brave? What inspired you to be brave? How can that experience help you today?

Press through. This is not forever. This is a season and seasons change.

What are some of the characteristics of the season you are in? What about this season do you like? What do you find uncomfortable or difficult? What do you wish you could change? What have you learned about yourself in this season? What will you take from this season into the next?

We are all flawed and beautiful. All of us, every one of us, imperfect and yet perfectly loved.

Acceptance and belonging are core needs of our humanity. Everyone wants to be accepted and needs to belong. We often hide the parts of ourselves we fear are unworthy of love so we won't face rejection. In doing so, we deprive ourselves of fully receiving all of the good the universe has to offer us out of fear our true selves won't be enough.

Are you willing to live life as a person who is decidedly imperfect but who is fully, completely, deeply loved and adored? Write about the freedom found in resting in a perfect love that accepts you just as you are. How does this love inspire you to love others? How does it help you with the ugly parts of life?

I prayed and asked God to hear me and He replied "Every heartbeat." And as I began to cry, tears falling from my face, He said "And I hear those too."

The biggest mistake we could ever make is to think we travel alone. We are never alone. Never. Dare in this moment to share a part of yourself with your Creator through written or spoken word. Tell Him how it feels to be you in this moment, at this time, and in this place. Allow Him to meet you at the place you most need to feel His love. Linger there, knowing there is no power on heaven or earth that could ever remove His love from you.

Big changes cannot happen without taking big chances. Those most successful are those most willing to fail.

Write about a time you experienced failure before succeeding. What did it take to get back up and try again? What did you learn in the process? What would you say to someone who is struggling with a failure?

When you are done playing it safe and allowing others to make you feel small, when the cost of settling is greater than the risk of daring, you have found the best version of you.

How can you face life today as the biggest version of you? What would that version of you look like? How would he or she talk? What goals and dreams would be front and center? What fears and insecurities would be left in the dust? Write your responses below.

Not all moments are moments we want to celebrate but they are all gifts.

Do you pause regularly to appreciate the gift of the minutes you are living? Take a few minutes to do so now and write your thoughts below.

When you have come to the end of who you are, you have found the beginning of who you can be.

Our unused potential is often discovered when we come to a place where our old ways of doing things simply won't get us through. What circumstances in your past have stretched you outside the limits of who you thought you could be? How have those experiences benefitted you?

Before your dreams can find wings, they have to find feet.

What are some practical steps you can take today towards reaching your dream? List them below. Now write about how you plan to use those completed actions to figure out your next steps. Any idea what those next steps might be? Write some thoughts below.

No circumstance, past or present, can define you without your permission. Any authority they hold they receive from you.

What circumstances have you authorized to speak for you? Be very specific. Have there been people in your life who told you those circumstances could speak for you? Are you allowing their opinion to give your past power? Are you willing to sever your identity with those circumstances and revoke their authority to make a statement about who you are?

Defining moments come not as we are assured of success, but in the willingness to step out towards our dream regardless of the outcome.

Uncertainty is one of the most difficult conditions for us humans to endure. We crave predictable outcomes and are very wary of any outcome we can't control. When we are reaching towards something we have never done before, we must be willing to give up that predictability and control.

What specific steps are you willing to take to step towards your dream even though there is no guarantee you will be successful? Who can you reach out to who has found success that might be a sounding board and guide for you? Reach out to them today. If you don't have a mentor, make finding one a top priority.

Few things are as difficult to overcome as the failure to comprehend one's worth. You cannot contribute what you do not believe you possess.

For you to give something of value to the world, you must believe you have value to give. Take a few minutes and make a list of five things about you that you truly value and appreciate. Reflect on those five things all throughout the day. Remind yourself of them often, especially when feeling anxious, fearful, or insecure.

Define your life in possibilities rather than limitations, have the courage to step towards them, and you will live what others only dream.

Decide today to be especially mindful of every opportunity that presents itself. Make a list of opportunities that arise all throughout the day. Opportunities to be kind, to be generous, to choose your response, to help someone, to take a step towards a dream, to start doing something, to stop doing something. It doesn't matter how big or small, just note each time you realize you've come across an opportunity. Count them up at the end of the day. Are you surprised at what you found? Return to this space and write about your experience.

If your internal climate isn't right, no amount of adjusting external conditions will matter. Success always begins within.

You may not be able to change all of the circumstances in your world that you find lacking or broken, but adjusting your attitude about them releases you from their tyranny. Shift your focus to you and how you are responding. Consciously choose to bring your best self front and center and take satisfaction in who you are choosing to be rather than in the details of the situation.

Write about a situation that is out of your control to change. Decide what attitudes, behaviors, and mindsets would result in peace for you. Write down some things you can do today to demonstrate those ways of being.

Perfection may beckon but it can never be caught. It cripples those who pursue it and blinds those who reach towards it.

Perfectionism is a joy stealer, a creativity killer, an intimacy annihilator. Everything about it is destructive. Perfectionism is a lie we buy into in a mistaken belief that if we achieve perfection, life will be fair and we will be loved. We know this isn't really true but we persist in chasing it anyway.

Take some time now to confront your perfectionistic self. Ask point blank what is it he or she believes will happen if perfection is achieved? What tragedies does he or she predict will befall you if you are not perfect? Be specific.

As you contemplate your answers, write out three small ways you can let go of perfectionistic striving today and free yourself of the lies perfectionism tells. Be specific. Acknowledge aloud that the real you, the imperfect you, is worthy of love and of belonging and commit to doing those three things today as your way of affirming this.

When the lies of limitations have ceased to be something we see as existing out there and have become something we believe we are, we surrender our destiny.

List five things you believe hold you back. For example, you may write "I am not wealthy". Now re-write those as observations of your experiences. For the above statement, you would write: "I have not yet had the experience of being wealthy". Or you could write "I don't have my college degree." Now re-write that as an observation of your experience by stating: "I haven't had the experience of obtaining my college degree yet."

How does this change your thoughts and feelings about your limitations?

The night, a liar; hope its test, fear its end.

When the night lies to you what does it say? What does hope say in response? What actions can you take in faith today to prove the night a liar? Write your thoughts below.

What wretched was, now beautiful become. Weakness made perfect in the strength of perfect love.

It is often the darkest, the most brutal, and the ugliest parts of our history that become the brightest and most brilliant lights and which offer hope to those around us. As we have the courage to heal and dare to believe in the redemption of even our deepest wounds, we give hope to other warriors wounded in battle.

Have there been people in your life who have given you hope through sharing their dark places? What did it feel like to know you were not alone? How can a dark experience you've had be a help to someone? Write your thoughts below.

Great victories are won a single step at a time. Choose an action that takes you towards your goal and is easily obtained. Repeat.

We love the excitement of big change but the truth is that substantial changes do not happen in one fell swoop. Rather, they are built brick by brick, step by step. Be committed to the process. Establish a system and work it daily. Like an artist laboring over each brush stroke, take joy in the small movements that create the big picture success you are after.

What steps in the process of creating your dream are you taking daily? Write about them below. How can you celebrate the little things that are necessary but not necessarily exciting?

here's some help

True commitment to a destination is not birthed from a certainty of arrival but from the conviction that come what may, you will persist.

You do not have to be sure you will get where you are going to be sure you will give it all you've got trying. Today, take note of each thing you are doing in pursuit of a better life, no matter how insignificant it may seem. In the space below write a thank you note to yourself acknowledging how much you appreciate the choice to take these steps when doing nothing would be so easy. Write about how proud you are of your determination and effort. Take deep satisfaction in the knowing you are giving your very best to this journey, regardless of the outcome.

Our rock bottom experiences teach us to look up, to get back up, to never give up.

Give thanks today for a rock bottom experience you have had. Acknowledge you made it through. Write down any blessings that have come from that experience and really savor their presence in your life.

If you are at rock bottom today as you read this, look up. What do you see? What possibilities lie ahead of you? What one step can you take today towards those possibilities?

That you fell is of little importance. That you got back up, now THAT is worth talking about.

Our focus is so often on how we messed up long after the event is done and over. Think today of a previous mistake that you've been holding on to. How did you get back up? What did that require from you? Think about what kind of person would have those qualities and would be able to get back up as you did? Maybe it wasn't pretty, but you did get back up. Are you defining yourself by your ability to rise back up, or by the events surrounding your fall? Write your thoughts below.

I can think of no more potent, sure path to healing than to find a hurt greater than your own and give yourself fully and diligently to easing it.

No matter where you are in life, you have something of value to give. Don't let the hardships you are facing convince you that you have no contribution to make. It is in stepping outside of our own pain to tend to the wounds of another that we find our own healing is made complete. Find a place, an organization, or a cause to give your time and efforts to. Return to this space and write about your experiences.

If you must label people, label them with potential, label them with the promise of good things yet ahead, label them with the power to overcome.

Someone today needs to hear you say you believe they have what it takes in every way to make it through to the other side of their storm. Speak life and words of hope to them today. Let them know that you see them as worthwhile, capable, and strong. Notice the emotions it stirs in you to speak out life over that person. Write about your experience below.

Many of the things we fear are nothing more than tomorrow's new normal. Insecurity and fear are part of the process of growth.

Recall a time that you were afraid of something that you later mastered. What convinced you to keep at it even though you were afraid? How can this knowledge help you manage any fears in your life today?

Guard your hope.

Hope is too precious a resource to be left unattended and too powerful an ally to be casually regarded. Do everything in your power to anchor yourself in hope. The kind of hope that propels you forward when everything and everyone around says you can't make it. The kind of hope that says—"No final curtain yet, this story isn't over." The kind of hope that bares its teeth at the darkness that seeks to devour and says "I've got more to give than what's yet been seen and more victories to win than battles to lose. Pull up a chair and get comfy, cause this story has just begun."

How can you allow hope to be an anchor for you today?

What a remarkable thing to turn one's heart towards joy in the very place where sorrow once reigned.

Healing is a process that takes us from what seems like endless pain to a new place of peace and knowing, a space where we find we can laugh again. Despite our deepest wishes, this process cannot be rushed. Little by little and bit by bit, we see the darkness begin to lift and splashes of joy begin to appear in what was once desolate and barren. In time, new life flourishes and we find the night has ended.

Write about a loss you have suffered. What did it feel like in the beginning when it first happened? How does it feel now? What helped you in your healing? What would you say to someone else going through a loss? Write your thoughts below.

The problem is we see the problem and we forget who we are.

Nothing is more devastating than disconnecting from a true awareness of who we are. When the storms hit hard, remember who you are—loved, able, capable, strong. They will go, you remain here on purpose for a purpose.

What practices can you develop to stay connected to who you are?
To your brilliance, your resilience, your compassion, your joy?

Start by writing about a hardship you've encountered and have overcome below. List all of the qualities you displayed in overcoming that circumstance. Allow that understanding to permeate your awareness.
All throughout the day seize opportunities to show the genuine you.

It is in moments of great discomfort, as we dare to stretch beyond the familiar, that we learn we are capable of more than we knew.

Everyone feels afraid, unworthy, incapable at times—everyone. It's what you do with that feeling that counts. The situation and setting may not be ideal and you may not feel like you are anywhere near ready, but less than perfect is as perfect as it gets. There's no more time for doubting, no room left for second guessing. Direct all of your energy at running the race. This is your time, your place. In the space below finish this sentence: " The situation is not perfect and still I will _____."

Pain is not an invitation to suffer. It is a signal you have outgrown your current way of living. Reach, stretch, grow. The work is hard, the rewards are many.

What area of your life is painful today? What would growth in that area look like for you? How can you begin today to grow in that particular part of your life? Write your thoughts below.

When lending your faith, make sure to send it in the direction of the solution rather than the problem, the provision rather than the need.

Everyone has faith in something. Either you surrender your faith to the problem or you release it in the direction of a solution. Be so very conscious today about what direction you are sending your faith. When we assume we don't have what it takes, we send our faith in the direction of the obstacles and the struggles. When we refuse to trust we send our faith out in the direction of what is painful instead of what is joyful. In the space below write out some of the ways you have been giving your faith. Decide to adjust anything that needs to be adjusted to allow your faith to serve your highest good.

When facing a setback those willing to trade their right to be disappointed for a belief in an opportunity disguised within usually find it.

Can you set aside your disappointment today and instead look for an opportunity for growth? Write down at least one situation where you have been let down and treated unfairly. You may indeed have a right to be upset but what would it feel like to choose instead to put your energy into caring for yourself? Write your thoughts below.

To see and be seen, to know and be known, to love and be loved is the core desire of every heart.

How can you see yourself today? What would it mean to really see who you are and acknowledge where you are right now? How can you honor and trust the sound of your own voice today? In what way can you show love to yourself today?

The most powerful gift you can give anyone is the gift of being truly present with them in their reality and choosing to be kind. Kindness changes everything.

With an awareness today of the deep longing in each human being to be seen, make it a point to reach out to someone who others look past and see through. Be intentional in your approach and set all judgments aside. Desire only to convey that you see them and that you acknowledge the commonness of your human existence. Write about your experiences below.

So you fell down. So it hurt. So here is the part where you show who you really are. You weren't meant to just look at the stars, but to reach them. Get back up even if the only reason you can find is to prove you still can.

What does your future self need from you today? Write your thoughts below.

Life is about making peace with what is while striving for what we dream can be. Success isn't achieving, it's flourishing wherever we are.

Just for today, set aside your focus on the big picture and on what you are hoping will come to be. You've given your goals and dreams full color and you are crystal clear on what they look like. Now shift your focus to all of the things that are present with you in your life today that you truly love and appreciate. Examine the landscape of your current life for all of the things which bring meaning and joy right here, right now. Make a list below.

You are not a problem to be fixed, you are a life to be lived. A beautiful, messy, heartbreaking, breathtaking, exhausting, exhilarating, perfectly imperfect life to be lived. There may be a deficiency in your understanding, a lack in your knowledge, a defect in your perspective, but there is not a lack, deficiency, or defect in you.

When faced with disappointments, do you see them as arising from a defect in you? Where did this sense of you being insufficient originate? Is this a belief you are willing to relinquish? Write a few thoughts about seeing yourself as enough in moments that lack what you had hoped for. What does it mean to be beautiful amidst the ugliness of life?

All that is required of us at any given time is to be the best we know to be, doing the good we know to do, with the information and resources we have available—period.

Take a deep breath. As you release it, let the demands of perfection flow out of you and dissolve into nothingness around you. Know with a deep and abiding trust that you have done all that you can do and it is enough.

Hope is not ignorant of suffering, nor of sorrow or loss. It is brazenly defiant in the face of it and staunch in its refusal to bow to it. Hope hears music in the starkest silence, downpours in raging drought, laughter in the deepest mourning. It knows nothing of resignation but is consumed with possibility.

What does your hope see and hear and speak today? Write about it below.

You can spend your entire life building walls to keep from being vulnerable only to end up in the most vulnerable position of all—alone.

It takes work to learn to trust, and it doesn't always end up the way we'd hoped. Still, being vulnerable and letting others see the real us is the only way to achieve intimacy. What one step can you take today towards lowering your walls and offering your true self to the world? Write it down in detail below.

There simply is no place where love cannot reach you. Brokenness isn't where your story ends, it's where it begins.

Too often we give the lowest point of our journey the authority to seal our fate. We give up right as we most need to press through. We offer our faith to the circumstance instead of to our ability to overcome.

In the space below write about a circumstance you've given authority over your future. Now write a letter from your future self to your present self detailing how you overcame that situation and how wonderful it was to have taken that area of your life back.

Now find a mirror, or use your phone, and say these words to yourself: "Shoulders back, head high. There are mountains to climb, battles to win, stories to write, and dreams to live."

The remarkable thing about the baggage we carry is that regardless of where and when we picked it up we can choose at any time to set it down.

What do you need to set down today? How can you exercise your power to choose to walk away from that today? How much lighter will you feel when you decide to no longer carry that baggage? How will freeing yourself of that load impact your life today? Write your thoughts below.

Walk when you can't run. Crawl when you can't walk. Find a way to keep moving forward. Courage is not quitting when you've every right to.

We sometimes believe that quitting will never seem justified. To the contrary, there will be times when quitting will actually seem the sane and logical thing to do. Courage means pressing on anyway in any way we can. Name one action you can take today, however small, to press on in a situation where you feel justified in giving up.

When we fail to appreciate where we currently are, it is impossible to accurately gauge what it will take to get to where we want to be.

What assets and resources are with you now that you are overlooking? Take a few minutes to fully recognize where you are and what you have at your disposal. Write your thoughts below.

Do not lend your belief to words spoken against you by those imprisoned by their own pain lest you join them in their suffering.

It may be difficult to see, but often those who hurt us the most are acting out of their own wounded places. Be careful not to join them in their woundedness by allowing their words or actions power in your life. Write about a time you were hurt by something someone said about you. How did you handle it? Does it have power in your life now? Can you see they are themselves wounded? How does this understanding help you heal?

Have the courage to be vulnerable. Be gentle when others are coarse. When given the choice to love or to judge, always choose to love.

Today give up your right to be annoyed, irritated, or upset and instead give compassion. Return to this space to record your experience.

When facing a situation that stretches you, seek counsel from someone who has long ago become comfortable navigating that same situation.

Going it alone is not heroic, it's a set-up for catastrophe. We need the insight and perspective of others and the benefit of their experiences. Even if we eventually reject their advice, we grow just by having expanded our thinking to include what they have known and seen.

Fear paints in shadows, bathing the landscapes of our lives in hues of catastrophes and sorrow as though they were the only possible outcome. The act of choosing hope breathes life into withered dreams and puts to flight the shadows fear has cast. It is impossible to choose hope and remain the same.

How has choosing hope changed you? Name one specific situation that you can choose hope in today and write about how that choice makes a difference to you and in you.

Keep moving towards what moves you. Give all you have even when it seems woefully inadequate. Your willingness to do so activates miracles.

We don't always know what the next leg of the journey will be. Sometimes the way is obscured and unclear. In those moments, it is critical that we keep moving towards what moves us, using our own passions and desires as a compass.

What lights you up? What makes you feel alive? Be specific. How can you move towards what moves you today? Write your thoughts below.

The wounds that cut deepest are those we've come to believe we deserve. Healing can only come when we no longer agree to carry that shame.

Many of us have entered into a contract with shame. We agree that we deserve our wounds, deserve the broken places, and agree to bear the shame. Shame is not the same as guilt. Guilt moves us towards better decisions in the future. Shame can't see we made a mistake, it perceives we are a mistake. We must break our contract with shame in our lives again and again if we are to be whole.

What areas trigger shame in your life? What step can you take today to name the mistake but refuse the perspective that you are a mistake? Write out what that looks like for you in the space below.

Faith is never reasonable and hope is rarely defensible. Both call upon us to abandon our concerns about fitting in, and dive headfirst into the business of living our convictions.

Write about the power found in defying the "norm". What benefit can you personally receive by refusing to settle for the status quo?

The greatest danger in allowing a situation to speak as to who we are is eventually it is our own voice that echoes the sentiment.

What situation has found its way into your thinking and way of being to such an extent that it now speaks for you? How can you reclaim the power of your own voice? Write your thoughts below.

Sometimes you find what you need most where you least expect to find it, among those you least suspect would have it.

Today, do something completely unexpected and out of the ordinary. Choose something you would never normally do and immerse yourself in the experience. Return to this space here to record your experiences.

The wounds most debilitating of all are those we've ignored for so long we've come to believe they are part of who we are. There is no perfect version of you living a perfect life waiting to be discovered somewhere. You have wounds, you have flaws, and still you are and always will be enough.

What hopes and dreams have you abandoned because of your wounds? What have you been putting off while waiting to be perfect? Be honest. What small action can you take today to abandon the myth of perfection and live the life you want to live? Write your thoughts below.

Just because the need showed up at your door doesn't mean you are the one to fill it.

It may be a hard truth to bite down on, but you are not God's answer to every problem that walks into your life. Sometimes the safest, sanest, wisest choice you can make to honor the need in someone's life is to let someone else meet it.

What do you need to say "no" to today? In the space below practice writing out several different ways that you can say no while respecting the need that has been presented and honoring your own need to pass on it.

Greatness and comfort cannot inhabit the same space. Getting there never involves staying here.

Name an area of your life today where you know you need to embrace being uncomfortable in order to grow. Write out one action you can take today to release your obsession with being comfortable and make a move towards your dream.

The greatest successes often lie hidden within the moments we least feel like rising to fight again. Warriors fall, victors get back up.

You may have fallen down a warrior, but you can rise a victor. Name a specific situation where you are declaring you will rise a victor. Now name one move you can make today towards getting back up.

There are those content to view the world as an ugly, cruel place. Then there are those willing instead to give themselves fully to the creation of a kinder, gentler, and more beautiful world.

What contribution can you make today towards making the world a more beautiful, kinder, gentler place? Write down the details below.

The most difficult part of clearing out any obstacle is coming to terms with what it is within you that allows it to be an obstacle.

Think of a situation where you are facing an obstacle and feel stuck, maybe even powerless. With brutal honesty today ask yourself what it is you are assuming that allows that particular situation to be so powerful, and you so powerless. What are you benefiting from that perspective? What needs to be adjusted? Who can you reach out to for help adjusting your perspective? Write your thoughts below.

We are broken and beautiful, empty and yet full of promise, crippled and still able to soar.

Our imperfections and wounds are not the whole story. We can be complicated messes full of insecurities with all sorts of reasons to fail and still be marching on toward health and wellbeing, towards powerful destinies, and towards breakthroughs and comebacks. Come to terms with your whole story today. Write the truth of your situation—the whole truth, and declare you and all of your messiness are headed for the victory lane.

It wouldn't be your gift if you weren't intended to use it.

What gift have you been neglecting out of an insecurity that you aren't good enough or it isn't important enough? Allow yourself to return to the joy of that gift and today practice it for the sheer enjoyment of interacting with that gift. Give no thought to the assessments or reactions of others. Rather, give yourself over fully to the gentle dance of that gift within you and offer it your full attention. Return to the space below to record your experiences.

You are not responsible for how others view you. You are responsible for how you view you. Get that straight and everything else falls into place.

Whose opinion do you need to leave behind today? Be specific and then set yourself free from the weight of their perspective.

Circumstances and situations cannot mold you nor shape you into anything you're not already willing to be—for better or for worse.

Name one specific way you can own your power today to shape a circumstance instead of allowing it to shape you.

We sculpt our reality from the clay of our expectations, and we can choose to paint it with the colors of our past or pick a whole new palette.

Are you coloring your today with pigments from your past? Wipe the slate clean and write about your new start below.

Beneath the fearful anxious thoughts flows a river of peace and knowing. To find it, go deeper and refuse to leave that place.

Find a quiet place and take a slow deep breath. Feel your chest expand. As you exhale, choose to feel at peace. Relax your body and as you breathe in again, notice how it is your choice to control the speed at which you breathe in and out. Choose a pace which causes you to feel calm. With each breath out, release a worry. Imagine it dissolving as it leaves your body. You can choose at any time to return to this state of mind and being and remain there as long as you like. Write your thoughts on this process below.

If you can learn something from a battle you have lost, you cannot call it a loss.

Do some research today on major successes that were preceded by major failures. Write a few examples below. What does that tell you about how you can benefit from your failures? Be specific.

If you're waiting for others to believe in you before you step out towards what you know is yours to do, you will never be who you came here to be. Though the gift of others believing in you is without question an asset, the gift of you believing in you is absolutely essential.

What one thing can you do today to demonstrate believe in yourself? Be specific and write the details below.

Don't invest in people for what they can give to you, invest in them for what they will one day be capable of giving to the world.

Who can you invest in today? How will you invest in them? What are you expecting from that interaction? What does it feel like to give with no thought of return? Write your thoughts below.

Our scars can either serve as a catalogue of past grievances or as a testament to battles fought and overcome. Those scars will one day remind you of the victory rather than the battle and bear witness to the miracle that became your story.

It takes courage to see the devastation brought to our lives as a marker indicating how we strong we are. It's much easier to get caught up in the "if onlys" and wanting to wish it all away but that only traps us in the event and strips us of our power. Who you were in the event matters far more than the event itself.

Take a few minutes to reflect on the times you have shown courage and strength in the face of adversity. Put the focus on you and fully own your power. You are what's important. Not what happened, but how you responded. Write your thoughts below.

If you're going to allow your failures to speak, let it be only to provide you with the information necessary to get back up and try again.

What information can your failures give you today that can help you in a current struggle? Write your thoughts below.

Did you ever consider there seems to be no path to where you want to go because the world is waiting for you to blaze one?

You are the world's only chance to experience you. Be confident in your ability to be who you need to be to carve out a way to your dream. Name one way you can show confidence in your vision today. Write your thoughts below.

How can we expect to receive that for which we have not yet made room? If your answer arrived today would you recognize it? Would you have a place for it?

Name something in your life you are hoping for. Have you prepared for it? Why or why not? How can you create a space in your life for it today? Write down the details below.

Despite what you may have been told to the contrary, your existence here is no accident. You matter, you are loved, you have a destiny. Go live it.

Today, pick something you've been meaning to get to and just go do it. No more planning, no more talking about it, just go do it. Return to write about your experiences here.

At some point, you have to ask yourself the question: Who benefits from you living as anything less than the brilliant light you were created to be? Answer: Not you, not those you love, and certainly not those whose lives you are here to touch.

Name an area you have been holding yourself back in out of fear of what others would think. How can you take action today to let your light shine? Be specific and write out the details below. Be who you are, shine like only you can.

Healing is both a destination and a journey. Grieving is the vehicle God gave us to get us there. Grieving is not a linear process. It comes in waves of highs and lows that, over time, subside and level out.

In the space below, give yourself permission to grieve in the ways that are most helpful for you. Write down some things that have been a help to you in the grieving process thus far. How can you do more of those, any of those, today? How can you demonstrate patience and compassion towards yourself during the ebbs and flows of the grieving process? Write your thoughts below.

In the midst of what's gone wrong, remind yourself of all that's gone right. Allow that to guide your focus, your emotions, and know that all is well. Walk certain of the great things yet to come. Know that your destiny is not determined by what you have, but by what you're willing to give.

Make a list of what has gone right. Be very specific. Now make a list of what you have to bring to the table. Every time you are tempted to look at what you don't have, go over that list. Find as many ways as possible to give of those qualities, characteristics, and gifts today. Return to this space to record your experiences.

Success is forged within our willingness to choose purpose over convenience with such persistence that it becomes a way of living.

What do you believe your purpose is? How is that inconvenient? In what way is your purpose asking you to stretch? Name one thing you can do consistently that is inconvenient for you but that aligns you with your stated purpose. Commit to doing that one thing each day for the next 14 days. Return to this space to record your experiences.

It's not a problem—it's a solution waiting to be discovered and you are so the one to do it.

We too often offer our faith to the experts and defer to the opinions of others over and over again, discounting our own abilities to find solutions. How can you honor your creativity and resourcefulness today? What problem can you bring your full authentic self to today? How can you demonstrate trust in your ability to figure out the best solution possible? Record your thoughts below.

The characters that show up, the scenes we find ourselves a part of, are all directly a result of the stories we tell about who we are.

Nothing matters more than the storyline we construct to describe who we are and what we can expect from life. Does your storyline fully reflect the possibilities of turnarounds, redemption, struggles made into strengths, shame set aside for true acceptance and appreciation of who you are?

How do you explain the wonderful things that show up in your life? What do you believe about the tragedies and heartaches that appear? Take a few minutes and write your thoughts below. Listen, really listen to the story you tell yourself about yourself. Realize you are the author and you have the authority to change anything that doesn't serve you well.

You can readily see how much you value your peace by how quickly you move to surrender it.

The absence or presence of things in our lives cannot bring us peace. They are transitory and impermanent. When we give them the power to give or take our peace we settle for a see-saw of up and down that is bound to changes in our lives. Peace is a choice to be at peace within ourselves regardless of what external circumstances are, or are not, shaping up the way we'd like them to.

What specific situations are you surrendering your peace to? Why? Are they worth your peace of mind? What steps can you take today to hold on to your peace in spite of the storms? How can you hold yourself accountable? Write your thoughts in the space below.

Sometimes the mountain moves. Sometimes the miracle is the strength to climb it and the gift of a view you couldn't have found any other way.

The way to our best life often looks very different than we imagined. We must give ourselves in trust that all is working together for our good in spite of appearances. There will be times when your faith that your dream can be will have nothing to stand on save faith itself---and it will be enough. Take a few minutes now to write words of faith to carry with you on your journey over, through, or around the mountains you encounter.

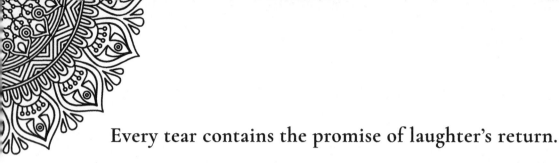

Every tear contains the promise of laughter's return.

Seasons of sorrow come to each of us. We must love ourselves enough to give ourselves the space to grieve. Healing takes time and we cannot rush the process. There is no right or wrong amount of time for healing to take place. It takes as long as it takes. In the space below give yourself permission to grieve, to mourn your loss, to appreciate the value of what was by fully acknowledging the empty space it left behind.

Sometimes it is impossible to articulate our dreams with words. We must shut out the world, close our eyes, slow our breath, and imagine the feeling of them. We must stay for awhile in silence, immersed in what it will feel like to accomplish the dreams written on our hearts and allow that feeling to feed the fire within.

Find a quiet place where you will not be disturbed. Breath slowly, deeply, intentionally. Allow your dreams to rise up within you. Stay with those images and feelings. Know they are within you because you are meant to live them fully. When you are finished, write down any thoughts in the space below.

The most insidious lies are those we fail to see as lies but believe as the realities of our world and of who we are.

The lie you believe becomes your truth and, once integrated, becomes the architect of your reality. Any belief that does not support your best and highest level of thriving and being, is a lie masquerading as truth. Any belief that strips away your value or assaults your worth is a lie which must be rooted out and extricated from your thinking so that you might be free to live your true identity.

In the space below, write down any belief which does not speak of your infinite, worth, value and ability to accomplish your purpose here on this earth. Speak aloud these words: " I revoke the authority of these lies in my life and offer myself fully to the restoration of the places within me that have been touched by them. In their place, I receive truth. Captive, go free."

The world needs you, the real you, to give what only you can give. Do not allow the expectations and demands of others to define what that is.

To do what you came here to do, you will have to get comfortable with disappointing others along the way. Stretch who you are, grow who you are, expand who you are, but never sell out, abandon, or compromise who you are. In the space below list some qualities about yourself that you are not willing to compromise. What values do you hold dear? What feeds your soul? Lights you up? As you go throughout this day, reflect upon how those qualities are essential to you being who you came here to be and give thanks for how they serve you and your purpose.

Etched onto our hearts and breathed into our souls, our dreams, when listened to, tell our future.

Find a quiet space and allow images of your dreams to flood your mind. Sit with them in silent reverence, letting them permeate your consciousness fully. What do your dreams tell you about your future? Write your thoughts in the space below.

There are chains not wrought of iron nor fashioned by human hands whose prisoners are kept only by the belief they must remain slave.

We often stay married to toxic and limiting beliefs which starve our soul and steal our vision because we are unaware it is a choice to remain linked with them. What three beliefs can you identify today that you know do not serve you well? Do you believe you can choose to let them go? What benefits are you receiving from hanging on to them? Be honest. Who can you connect with who has successfully divorced themselves from limiting beliefs that you could reach out to for guidance and support?

You've been here before, you know what to do, you have what it takes. Shoulders back, head high. This is your time.

In the face of present trouble, we often forget how well we've navigated treacherous ground before. We must cultivate a mindset that integrates our previous victories and use them as platforms to reach even higher.

In the space below, write about a time you were able to navigate a difficult season successfully. What are the highlights and the takeaways from that experience? What energy and wisdom can you pull forward into your present situation? Use the space below to write your thoughts and detail specific strategies you can apply to your world today from that past experience.

Being brave rarely feels like being brave. Do it anyway.

Find a mirror or use the camera on your phone. Throw your shoulders back and lift your head high. Look yourself square in the eye and say out loud, "I am brave!".

We often say we "can't" and speak as though it is fact. What we are actually saying is we don't *believe* we can. There is a difference.

Think of an area in your life where you have felt defeated and overwhelmed. In the space below complete the sentence "I can't _____" by filling in what it is that you have felt unable to overcome. Now add "but I am willing to learn how now." What one step could you take today towards learning what you need to know to change that "can't" to a "can"?

Difficulties are temporary situations that need your permission to take up permanent residence.

Very few things in our lives are permanent. Change is the ever constant in life. Name a way you can frame a current difficulty as a temporary situation. What will your life look like when that trouble has ended? Write the details below.

Confidence is not the absence of doubt and fear. It's moving forward anyway, dragging your insecurities kicking and screaming (as they most assuredly will be) with you as you go.

Don't get caught up waiting for fear to dissipate or fade away before taking the action you need to take. It won't. The good news is, you can move anyway. In the space below, write something you've been putting off, hoping you could get to a place where you would no longer be afraid. Now write down how you can take action today, regardless of what your fears and insecurities are saying. Return to this space to record your experience and to celebrate your actions.

If you quit now, the stuff wins and the stuff was never intended to win. You are intended to win and destined to succeed in every way.

In the space below list some of the "stuff" that you feel is hindering you. Look at each item and ask if you are willing to let that particular item decide your destiny. Realize you may not yet know what you need to know to beat that situation, but you can learn it. Remind yourself that you are here for a purpose and created to fulfill it.

Now make a list of all the resources you could employ to learn more about the situations you are facing and how to overcome them. Choose one and begin today.

Those things, circumstances, and events that are holding us back would have zero power to do so if we were not holding onto them.

Consider that it is not what is holding you back but what you are holding onto that is the issue. What would letting go look like for you? Write your thoughts in the space below.

The past holds no capacity for creativity. Only by living fully in this moment right now can we find the power to create, to shape, and to forge.

With everything you have this day, release your power, your brilliance, your knowledge, and your passion into the present. What has been, has been. Many of your past circumstances will return as benefits to you at a future time, but they must be left where they are now so you can fully live today.

Your future self is counting on you to breathe in the moment with you now, to infuse it with joy, to fill it with peace, to love yourself fully and completely just as you are. There will never again be a chance to live the moment with you now. Treasure it.

In the space provided write words of gratitude for what you find with you this very minute, for the possibilities this present moment gives birth to. Immerse yourself in awe of the wonder of drawing your breath, feeling your heartbeat, and adoring the space in this universe that you, and you alone, have been given to fill.

IN COMPLETE AWE and with deepest gratitude

I acknowledge the gift of the presence of the following people in my life without whom this book would still be just a dream within me:

To my brother Jeff, thank you for your stubborn insistence that my parachute would open. It did, and what a view!

To Amanda Mary, thank you for trudging through the muck with me and for the gift of your creative genius, for calming me down and pointing me forward. I could not have done this without you!

To Claudia and Alcides, la belleza de tu espíritu es incomparable, tu bondad y compasión nunca terminan. Estoy eternamente agradecido por ti.

To Joy Kramer, words cannot express how your bright light and sweet spirit have impacted my life. Thank you for your unwavering belief in me. Most of all, thank you for sanctuary amidst the changing winds.

To my five amazing children, Jessica, Joshua, Andrew, Sara, and Noah, you are, and will always be, my every heartbeat. You inspire me daily to dream bigger and reach higher. Thank you for putting up with all of the insanity. Love you fiercely!

53637150R00209

Made in the USA
Columbia, SC
19 March 2019